A LIFETIME OF
RUG-HOOKING

DORIS EATON

NIMBUS
PUBLISHING LTD

Nimbus Publishing Limited
3731 Mackintosh St, Halifax, NS B3K 5A5
(902) 455-4286 nimbus.ca

Printed and bound in Canada

Author photo: Peter Barss / peterbarss.com
Cover & Interior design: Kathy Kaulbach, Touchstone Design House

Library and Archives Canada Cataloguing in Publication

       Eaton, Doris, 1928-
       A lifetime of rug hooking / Doris Eaton.

       ISBN 978-1-55109-846-3 (pbk).
       ISBN 978-1-55109-829-6 (bound)

1. Rugs, Hooked—Atlantic Provinces. I. Title.

TT850.E28 2011   746.7'4   C2011-900041-5

We acknowledge the financial support of the Government of Canada through the Book
Publishing Industry Development Program (BPIDP) and the Canada Council, and of
the Province of Nova Scotia through the Department of Tourism, Culture and Heritage
for our publishing activities.

DEDICATION

To my ever-patient husband, Ron, and our family for their love and support over the years; to a special rug-hooking group who've been there for me for over thirty years; to my many friends for their affection and encouragement; to Heather Horsfall, who saw a book in my rugs and their stories and saw to it that I got started; to Joan Sinclair, who "found me" in my volumes of letters and pictures and notes and clippings and whose knowledge and expertise kept me focused and led the way to a publisher; and to Peter Barss, who declared he would be my own personal photographer and who dedicated much time and talent to the quality of my book.

Mary Sheppard Burton, who wrote the definitive book for rug hookers and fibre artists, *A Passion for the Creative Life: Textiles to Lift the Spirit*, became a lifelong friend and mentor and fell in love with Nova Scotia when she came to visit. She wrote a wonderful tribute to me when she gave me her book:

"Your work is powerful and dramatic. Those who read my book will find this true. You have expressed through color and wonderful design the magnitude of your art. We learn so much from you. Like my dear friend Joan [Moshimer] you open our eyes that we might see with our heart. I love you! – Mary"

When all of religion and philosophy and indeed life itself comes together,
the most we can hope for is to become the best that we possibly can,
each in our space here on earth, in our age and time of life.
In all humility, I have tried to do my best with whatever talents I possess.
I aspire to no great heights, just to do my best in my time and place.

D. E.

CONTENTS

FOREWORD

When I first started hooking rugs, twenty-one years ago, it was clear to me that there was one woman I needed to see. That woman was Doris Eaton. Even my untrained eye told me that whatever she was doing, it was pretty special. Her rug, *My Word,* from 1989, was one of the first of hers I had seen, and I got lost in it. When I turn over my pillow to the cool side at night, I still think of that rug, and the word "abilene" that she hooked into it. The expressiveness in her work captured my heart. Her rugs reached out to me and I in turn reached out to her.

I heard she was attending the Nova Scotia Rug Hooking School in Truro, and I went there to meet her, to show her my rugs, and we have had a friendship ever since. Her only advice to me then was "Keep doing what you are doing." Looking at the collection of work in this book, this is clearly advice that Doris followed herself. Whether the journey was through tidal pools and gardens, into houses, or towards friends, she just followed, and trusted that she was here to make rugs.

Doris made a habit of showing up to work on her rugs, keeping a promise to herself and her art for a lifetime. What more does any artist have to offer the world; what more could she give? I love her philosophy of not trying to achieve great things but focusing on doing your best in your time and place—imagine that. She has taken that philosophy and used it to create a body of work that has great depth. Her rugs are imaginative and expressive, exquisite and beautiful.

When I look at this book, it is clear that she has added beauty to the world. She has helped make rughooking meaningful and gracious. Doris herself is gracious, unassuming, and kind. She has been supportive to many rug hookers over the years, helping them make their own work more beautiful, helping them build a community to carry on this Atlantic Canadian tradition. She has helped define and shape contemporary culture in Atlantic Canada, making for us a place where handwork and artwork can mean the same thing.

Deanne Fitzpatrick
April 2011

A LIFETIME MOSAIC:
ARTISTRY IN THE WORLD OF CRAFTS

I'd like to share some of the experiences, insights, and creative joy I have enjoyed in my lifetime. As I look back, small things have made big differences and given me direction. I believe the small incidents that happen to us all when we are children help steer our courses for the rest of our lives.

My interest in rug hooking began when I was very young; I have been very involved in it for much of my life. I was born in Boston City Hospital, of Canadian parents. My dad had gone to the Boston States as a young man to seek his fortune, and my mother was visiting her aunt, who ran the boarding house where this young man was staying.

After their marriage, they were taking in a movie one night and won the door prize being offered by the theatre. It was a piece of land in Norwood, Massachusetts and as soon as they could afford it, they built their new home there. So instead of being brought up in a city, my sisters and brother and I were raised on the outskirts of a lovely New England town, amidst fields lined with lichen-covered stone walls, with ponds where we fished and caught pollywogs, and with woods and streams to explore to our hearts' content.

I'm so thankful that my parents and teachers did so much to encourage any natural talent I possessed. I enjoyed excellent art courses in all grades, and wonderful supplies and equipment, including lino cutting tools and a small hand press for block printing. Our instruction covered fine

art and commercial art, and in junior high school all of Friday afternoon was devoted to a wide range of art activities including my favourites: Indian beadwork, flower arranging, and basket making.

I was also lucky because Saturday art classes were offered at the Massachusetts School of Art in Boston. My parents gave me the fare each Saturday all winter to travel to Boston. Drawing and painting classes went until three o'clock; I was back home in time for supper, which was often after dark in the wintertime. It was a ninety-minute trip each way, and involved my taking a bus to Jamaica Plain, then a streetcar with a transfer to another street. I marvel at

this now; no schoolchild would be allowed to travel alone like that today. But I remember how important it was to me. I still have the sketchbooks full of bits and pieces of the people and places I drew while travelling back and forth on all those trips.

After high school there was no doubt in my mind where I wanted to continue my education—the Massachusetts School of Art. I thrived during those years. Although the facilities were older and low key, the school had an excellent teaching staff and what I learned in those years has enriched my entire life.

When I go back as far as I can remember, what comes to mind is my first pleasure at putting together colours and textures. My grandmother had a friend named Mrs. Tupper, who was a seamstress. Mrs. Tupper saved scraps of brightly coloured fabric in a shoebox and brought these to my sisters and me each summer, to use for making doll's clothes. I wasn't much interested in playing with dolls, but I did love making all the velvets and silks and prints and laces into little quilts and shawls for my younger sisters to wrap their dolls in. This was the beginning of my lifelong interest in colour, design, and fabric.

My father's family was from Walden, Nova Scotia, inland from Mahone Bay, and my mother's home was in Canning in the Annapolis Valley, near Cape Blomidon. When my brother and sisters and I were let out of school for the summer months, my mother had us all packed and ready for a two-day trip to Nova Scotia to visit relatives and friends along the South Shore and in the Valley.

There are so many memories of those wonderful summer months—picnics, beach combing along the Bay of Fundy, piling our grandmother's winter wood in an unused back room, collecting eggs from her small flock of chickens, and picking blueberries in Mr. Brown's pasture all day, with egg sandwiches for lunch. On occasion we trekked to town, about an hour away along a dirt road, to do a few errands and pick up meat from the local butcher for our supper.

I had graduated from high school, and I left my job when my dear grandmother became ill and came to Nova Scotia to take care of her. Her youngest son, my uncle Eddie, lived with her, but he had a job to go to and she needed twenty-four-hour care. Eddie had been in the Royal Canadian Air Force during the war, and when he came home, he worked on a farm in lower Canard. Ron Eaton was the farmer's son, and

they worked together and became fast friends.

And all this came together when I came into the picture. Ron proposed and I accepted, and we looked forward to the quality of life farming offered us and our children. We wanted a family and I thought having a litter was a good idea—to get it all over with at once—but I had to settle for having our children one at a time. We had five children over the next eight years and the very fact that I was so busy being a farm wife and mother gave me the next direction in my life.

Because I had no time for what I considered artistic expression, I became totally frustrated. It seemed I was forever washing diapers and making formula. Our home was decorated to the nth degree, and the children were dressed in frills and flounces, mostly made by my mother-in-law and me. I grew beautiful flowers and arranged them to my heart's content. I sang in the church choir, presided over the Women's Institute, and became a gourmet cook. But something was still missing. I needed to get back to making art.

In desperation I devised what I called "My Wednesday." It was a day all my own. The children spent time in their playpen or in their rooms with toys or books, or they spent a day with Grammy. The meals were prepared the day before; friends were asked not to phone and my husband didn't interrupt. This gave me my Wednesday, a wonderful space of time each week just for me. It saved my life and kept me on track with my artistic endeavours. It worked so well that I kept to that regime all the years our children were home, and beyond. I continue with "My Wednesday" to this day.

When I heard of a rug-hooking teacher who had moved to nearby Wolfville, I invited her to come to our Women's Institute (WI) meeting

to demonstrate rug hooking. Well, that did it! I was literally hooked!

I had enjoyed learning so many crafts over the years, but rug hooking became the medium for my artistic expression that transcended all others. The process is quite simple. Take a strand of material and pull it through a backing to form loops on the surface, which pack together to eventually become a rug or wall hanging. It takes fifteen minutes to learn to hook, but a lifetime isn't long enough to explore the possibilities of colour and texture and design it can offer.

Mrs. Edna Withrow had studied rug hooking in her native Ontario and taken courses in Massachusetts under Pearl McGown. She brought an expertise and a beautiful sense of colour to her craft unlike anyone else in Nova Scotia at that time.

When she came to our WI meeting to demonstrate rug hooking, she brought the most beautiful rugs she had made, and showed us how she cut wool rags into strips on a little machine clamped to a table, and how she dyed swatches and shaded flowers. It brought back a flood of memories for me and solved the mysteries of how my grandmother's rugs were made. Before this, I only knew my grandmother's rugs as the pattern stamped on burlap, and then the next summer the finished mat, but I never saw the work that took place in between.

Mrs. Withrow's rugs were of the finest workmanship with subtle shadings, and were like exquisite tapestries. In comparison, my grandmother's rugs had been quite crude with the pattern outlined in black, the roses hooked in two or three shades of whatever red wool she had available, and the leaves in two shades of green, with all that wool cut by hand.

Our WI group was so enthusiastic that evening that we decided then and there to form a class. Six of us

chipped in a few dollars and we bought our first cutter. For me it was the beginning of a lifetime passion. Eventually all my knitting, crocheting, and other craftwork were dropped by the wayside and hooking and painting became my chosen outlets for my artistic talents.

Mrs. Withrow taught us not only to hook, but to take new material and dye it into perfectly graduated swatches to shade lovely flowers and fruits. She also taught us to dye over "found" material to achieve beautiful effects and to use to best advantage the woolen materials we would find at rummage sales.

She brought a refinement to the craft that was so new and different. With her knowledge of newer methods and beautiful colouring, it opened up a whole new world to those who already hooked or who remembered it fondly from their childhood. She travelled all over Nova Scotia teaching everyone who wanted to learn a more sophisticated approach to this heritage craft of rug hooking.

Many rug hookers in Nova Scotia today were students of Edna Withrow and remember her so fondly. She gave us a treasure it would be hard to place a value on. I have met no one who can match her exquisite sense of colouring and the knowledge to use those colours to their best advantage.

I took many courses from Mrs. Withrow, plus I travelled to the US for more classes. After that I felt reasonably qualified to become a teacher. I started teaching in 1970 and taught all over Nova Scotia for the next ten years. I hope I've encouraged uniqueness and individuality in rug hooking. I love what I do and I hope this rubs off on others. Of all the rugs I've seen over the years, the ones I remember are the original designs. This is what I try to impress on anyone I talk to about rug hooking.

Of course rug hooking did not begin with Mrs. Withrow. The Maritime area of Canada is fortunate in that it has a unique heritage in rug hooking. For many generations people have hooked rugs during the long winter evenings in homes often remote from their neighbours and the nearest towns. Usually the maker sat by the warmth of the fire working worn-out clothing into colourful images using a burlap feed bag for a backing. Sometimes neighbors were invited in and rug-hooking bees were enjoyed by all.

Hooks were made of kitchen utensils or farm tools, fashioned with wooden handles, which could be shaped to fit the user's hand more comfortably. Some old hooks exist which are intricately inlaid or have ornate ferrules. A few were fine and slender, but most were quite stubby with a wide shank which opened up the burlap when it was punched through, making it easier to draw the hand-cut rag to the surface.

The loops formed in this way have produced an art form that is marvellous to all who see it. Women took great pride in perfect, even rows hooked so precisely that it was hard to believe they had been done by hand. Perhaps nowhere did this reach such a peak of perfection as it did in Lunenburg County, Nova Scotia. The ethnic background of many of the people in this area was German and their practical hooked rugs were of geometric designs, with the loops placed evenly in every other hole in the backing, hooking alternate rows carefully, so that the result was perfectly aligned rows of loops in both directions. If flowers were in the centre, they were quite simple with their background hooked in this very precise way. It's easy to distinguish these rugs from those of other areas in the Maritimes.

The main reasons for hooking mats were to wipe dirty feet at the

back door when coming in from doing barn chores, or to cover drafty floors. They were also a way to use up wool clothing that was worn out; thriftiness was a virtue in those hard times. Waste not, want not.

At some point beauty crept into this process, perhaps in a primitive way at first, but those simple mats have become the wonderful folk art rugs we collect today. Gradually the hooking craft became more sophisticated. A machine was invented to cut material into very fine strips, and fine burlap became available by the yard. It was now possible to intricately shade flowers, work out scenes, and even imitate oriental rugs, with beautiful results.

Dyeing woolen fabric using natural materials, such as lichens and bark, involves gathering these materials and using specific mordants to set the colour. Although the colours are beautiful and "earthy," this process takes time. Commercial dyes come in many colours and can be combined for an infinite range of shades. There are also many, many dye books with endless possibilities for perfect, even dyeing or splotchy, creative dyeing for special effects.

Today, rug hooking is enjoying phenomenal growth here in Nova Scotia. We have a very active rug-hooking guild and our major function each year is the annual Nova Scotia Rug-Hooking School. There are now many women who enjoy

the creative pleasures of producing artistic pieces and enjoy the finished product, either as rugs for the floor as our grandmothers used them, or as wall hangings, seat covers, or for display in any number of ways.

Women of today still enjoy the social side of rug hooking when they pick up their portable frames and basket of wool strips, pack a lunch, and go to a neighbour's to spend the whole day hooking with others in the community. The discussions around the hooking frames cover the intricacies of the various designs, the dyeing methods used to produce beautiful colours, and ways to work out the problems unique to each design. Each woman works creatively to perfect her design ideas and colour sense. I started hooking when I was thirty-three. I am now eighty-two. I've seen the growth of the craft in a most unique way. In one year alone I taught 150 people how to hook!

I think my own rugs have been well received because they are original. I hook an average of three rugs a year, and have hooked four stair runners and a family rug that took seven years to complete. I enjoy trying out new ideas and pushing this craft in new directions. I hope I'm making a difference.

There is a quote I refer to a lot that was shared with me years ago by my friend Mary Sheppard Burton. It's found in the book *The Art Spirit* by Robert Henri:

I have no sympathy with the belief that art is the restricted province of those who paint, sculpt, make music or verse. I hope we will come to understand that the material used is only incidental; that there is an artist in every man; and that to him the possibility of development and of expression and the happiness of creation is as much a right and as much a duty to himself, as to any of those who work in the especially ticketed ways.

A Word on Materials

I have almost always used recycled wool or "found" materials in my rugs, with very few exceptions. This was the tradition of Nova Scotian mats and I truly believe in it. My grandmother saved her prettiest wools for her front room rugs. The back door mats were duller colours, and their patterns were plain stripes or squares.

A plaid or tweed material adds a great deal of texture to a hooked rug, because it blends interesting colours or it gives minute contrast in narrow strips when they're finely cut and added to the pattern. I also find that sweaters add another effect, either cut along the ribbing in a fairly wide strip that forms a tube as it stretches, unravelled and used in double strands, or paired with another fibre for a special effect. This use of "other" fibres is innovative and exciting because you never know what the result will be. I do try to hook with woolen fibres or fabric if the piece is to be a rug for the floor. The art rugs being produced today will probably never be walked on, so we don't have to be as restrictive with their materials.

I always use a linen backing to hook into, because it wears longer than anything else. Our daughter repairs rugs, and the only thing that ever wears out in an old rug is the burlap it was hooked on. The hooking may still look good, but because burlap is adversely affected by water and light, it becomes dry and brittle, rendering it beyond repair. Therefore, I always use linen for my rugs and wall hangings. And I think I'm safe in guaranteeing them for two hundred years.

We are very fortunate in the area of Nova Scotia where I live to have Frenchy's outlets selling good quality used clothing and fabrics, and sometimes brand new fabrics. I also find woolen fabric at other used clothing shops, at church rummage sales, or from friends with moth-eaten wool to give away. I have become quiet proficient at over-dyeing what comes to hand to get just the colour I'm looking for. Therefore, I don't buy new wool and it is fair to say that I use recycled woolen materials almost exclusively in my work, as my grandmother would have done.

The only exceptions to that in this book are the *Family Saph Rug* and the pixilated *My Friendly Garden*. These two rugs needed consistent fabric for precision hooking. The Saph Rug is of #3 cut wool and the Garden is of #4 cut.

As spinners and weavers become more prolific in our area, I love adding their textures and colours to my work. I combine threads of fine yarns with woolen fabrics for interesting effects. I've used treated kelp (seaweed), cut while moist, as well as suede and leather. But unless there is a specific notation listed under a rug's name, it has been hooked using recycled woolen fabric.

A Treasure Trove
of Unique Designs

J. Worthington Winthrop III

33" × 25"
Recycled and found wool fabric,
roving on linen backing
2001

I wanted to do a hooking about my grandmother Pash (short for Patience) because she was one of my favourite people. When we were schoolchildren, the absolute highlight of each year for my sisters and brother and I was going to stay with our grandmother in Canning, Nova Scotia, for the entire summer holiday.

To my mother she was "Mum," but for us, her grandchildren, she was always "Pashy." My grandmother loved to hook, so the best gift my mother could bring her every year was a mat pattern printed on burlap, new from the "Boston States."

Because hooking was traditionally a winter activity, I only saw the pleasure on Pashy's face when she unfolded the pattern we'd brought and considered what materials she would need to make it. Then she would stow the pattern away in a trunk bulging with rags, to await the long days of winter when she worked on her hooking projects.

When we came back the following summer, a beautiful new mat would adorn the living room floor, made from the pattern we'd brought the year before. My grandmother hooked her "best rags" into parlour mats; she saved her "old rags" for the back door mats. Her rags came from old clothes such as Stanfield's woolen underwear. She also recycled Humphrey pants, a thick wool pant that men wore when working outdoors in the winter. She mostly used the colours as she found them, but if she needed something different she would use Tintex and

Rit dyes and onion skins to create new colours.

I remember one summer Pashy was just itching to get started on a particularly lovely hooked rug pattern of roses, leaves, and scrolls that we had brought her. Before we left at the end of August, she got out her coloured rags. She rooted around in the cubbyhole under the stairs and unearthed four narrow pieces of wood, which she clamped together at the corners to make a frame. By now I was old enough to handle a pair of scissors, so she allowed me to cut some rags so she could begin hooking. She laced the pattern we'd brought into the frame, balanced the frame on the backs of kitchen chairs, and I finally got to see how she hooked a rug. That was all. But it was enough.

I loved her rugs and every summer I looked forward to seeing what she'd created over the winter. But Pashy never understood what was so great about them—to her, they were just dusty old things that covered the wide cracks in her floorboards. She threw them over the clothesline every spring and beat them with a wire paddle until clouds of dust drifted over the wet grass.

Then one memorable year when we arrived for the summer, all the rugs were gone—the lovely ones from the parlour and the worn ones from the kitchen, too. They'd all been replaced by shiny new linoleum and Pashy was delighted because the linoleum was so easy to sweep and keep clean. But I was devastated. All her wonderful mats—gone. A salesman had come by that spring and offered to trade her old hooked mats for brand new linoleum for the dining room, kitchen, and parlour floors, and she had jumped at the chance.

Many years later, I attended Deanne Fitzpatrick's hooking workshop because I saw something in Deanne's work that moved me. How could a few bold loops and her spontaneous approach evoke such strong feelings? When I stood back to study her work I was amazed how these loops of wool became such effective landscapes, and the people in them became so real. In her workshop Deanne asked me to think about the person my grandmother was and it brought back all these memories of Grandmother Pash.

She often wore a sweater, so I hooked her in her sweater. She always wore an apron, her hair was snow white, and her shoes were interesting because she had to cut slits in them to make room for her bunions and big toes. (She did this even with brand new shoes.)

Pash

33″ × 25″
Recycled and found wool fabric,
roving on linen backing
2001

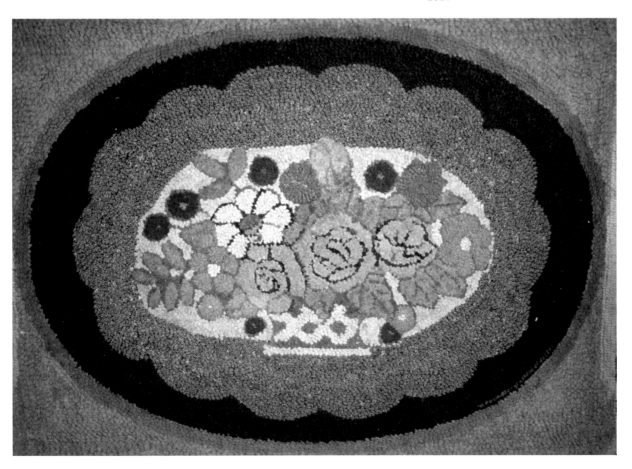

When my uncle was away at war, Pashy had a flock of egg-laying hens that she kept to earn extra money. She fed those chickens at the same time every day and they sang to her when she collected their eggs. Her eight chickens spent their free-range days in the yard and came hurrying to her when they heard the feed rattling in the can.

She also took in laundry as another way to make money in those hard times. On washday she had to heat the water in a big copper boiler on top of the woodstove. When it was hot enough the water went into a large wooden washtub with a handle that went back and forth to agitate the clothes. After rinsing everything in a galvanized tub, Grandmother hung the laundry on her clothesline, which was stretched between three apple trees and raised in the middle by a forked pole. She had a large quince tree by the back door of her house and she made the most delicious quince jelly imaginable. She mixed the quince equally with apples to produce the pectin needed for the jelly.

Working from an old photograph, I first drew her feeding the chickens in front of the house with all of its doors and windows. When I reflected upon what was most important in this story of my grandmother, I realized that the house detracted from what I wanted to say. So I replaced the house with apple trees, the clothesline, the quince tree, and Cape Blomidon. I had already hooked in the outhouse behind a lattice fence on the left. I wanted to keep that little outhouse because it was papered inside with cartoons from the *Boston Sunday Globe* that my mother saved each week and delivered to Grandmother on our summer visits, rolled up inside the mat patterns.

My brother Bernie and sister Jean memorized these cartoons and acted them out for Pashy, to her delight. One line in particular from "Joe Palooka"—"My man, the lemon squeezer must win to uphold my prestige"—must have been my line in the production, because I remember so well the haughty dame who spoke it.

J. Worthington Winthrop III is Pashy's cat. He came all the way from Parrsboro, Nova Scotia, and he followed my grandmother everywhere.

The Old Gent Himself

Approximately 42″ diameter
Hooked of wool rags on linen
1992

The Old Gent Himself was the name of a great old bird that my husband and I were told was a "turkey duck," a rare Nova Scotia breed particularly meaty and good for market. Someone was pulling our leg. He was a Muscovy, a rather common breed, but that made him no less interesting. I think he was ancient when we got him—hence his name—but he was a family favourite and had the run of the yard when we ran a bed and breakfast in Petite Rivière, on the South Shore of Nova Scotia.

Our grandchildren thought the Old Gent should take a wife. On my husband Ron's birthday in May, they gave him a female duck to keep the Old Gent company. When the heavy spring rains came, the Old Gent was swept off his favourite rock and into the brook that ran by our back door. He went down that brook and into Petite Rivière, floating out toward the sea, before finally coming safely to rest in some bulrushes at a house across from the fire department.

Meanwhile, we looked everywhere for him, and after two weeks decided he was gone for good. Then, one afternoon, I walked to our local store with our grandchildren and we saw a duck that looked like ours. We asked the lady of the house about the duck in her yard. She knew it must be someone's pet, but didn't know how to find the owner. Each day at suppertime he waddled up to her back door, pecked at the screen, and was treated to a hamburger bun or a piece of bread. She had named him Moses because he was in her bulrushes.

We called Ron, and he came with his bottle of rum, and poured about a triple on the bird's food. Moses ate it all. Well, the duck could get up on his tiptoes and flap his wings, but he couldn't get airborne. The man of the house handed Ron a dip net (for fishing), and we had him.

We brought him home and put him on the lawn. He staggered into a tree, and wove his way through the yard and in through the barn door. His mate was waiting for him, and must have forgiven his wayward ways, for they had a lovely little brood of ducklings. We re-named our duck Moses and found Moses's wife's name, Zipporah, in the Bible. That was the name we gave his mate.

When I came upon a photo of our old duck a few years later, it brought back a flood of memories about him and his mate, his broods, his orneriness, and the lovely brook he enjoyed. As I sat reading beside that brook, with its babbling noise drowning out all other sound, I was inspired. There was a rug in that story. The idea for *The Old Gent Himself* was born. Perhaps this is what is best about the rug-hooking craft—telling a story. As we hook a rug, we relive our memories, and then later we do so every time we look at our creation.

I wanted a random shape for the rug of *The Old Gent Himself*, so I put my piece of linen on the floor. Standing in the centre, I leaned over with my marker at arm's length, turning as I went, and drew an oddly shaped circle. I liked the result. It may sound weird, but it was just right for the rug I wanted to create.

Now I had the outside dimension and I drew the design freehand, using my photograph as a guide. I cut my woolen material by hand or used a #6- or #8-size cut for the entire rug. I outlined the shapes in the image, as my grandmother would have done, but not in black, as her choice would have been. Instead, I used a deeper colour value of the flowers, the leaves, the rocks, and other shapes in my design. The effect was just what I wanted.

Every rug presents different problems and the creative fun comes from finding solutions. The rug of Zipporah displays her waiting for the Old Gent on his rock in the brook. In this hooking I used my grandmother's traditional black lines and restricted palette.

I designed this piece first as a small watercolour painting, using pen and black ink in concert with the watercolours. The original painting was given to a friend in Japan. *The Old Gent Himself* was given to a visitor and flown to Vancouver as her new pet. *Zipporah* hangs in my living room.

Zipporah

36″ × 36″
Recycled wool fabric, #5 cut
2001

'Tis Happy Hour When Eddie Comes To Call

65" × 21"
Pencil roving, dog's fur, yarns, wool fabric,
#6 cut on linen backing
2005

This rug is about our neighbour, Eddie. Eddie is 80 years old, 110 pounds, and a very positive man.

Our dog, Taz, loves him. He waits for Eddie to arrive carrying his two store-bought cookies and he won't leave Eddie alone until he gets that second cookie. Eddie has many problems in his life, but when he comes to call he arrives with a new story or a song or a ditty like "You picked a fine time to leave me, Lucille."

Each day he announces his new word for the day, like "overwhelming" or "fantastic." His new word of the day is always positive. He comes three times a week to visit at Ron's happy hour, around four o'clock. Ron pours himself a drink of Bacardi's Light and 7-Up, and he and Eddie sit across from each other at the kitchen table.

Ron's freshly baked bread is often cooling on the rack beside the fridge. They chat about old times and old ways, who's who and what's what in our neighbourhood. They talk about Eddie's job as a truck driver and working on the lake boats in Ontario and picking blueberries in Maine. Ron reminisces about his days of farming in the Annapolis Valley. They natter away until the clock strikes five, when Ron gets up from the table to put the potatoes on for supper. Eddie knows this is his signal to go home.

While Eddie and Ron natter, I'm sitting in the living room hooking, as I am most afternoons. Surrounded by books, music, stained glass, and hooked rugs, it is a special place. I get lost in my hooking.

One-third of our house is my studio. My drafting table, storage drawers, a light table, and my Bolivar cutters are surrounded by shelves full of an incredible supply of Frenchy's wool. The clothes I've discovered at Nova Scotia's discount clothing phenomenon, Frenchy's, have been torn apart by Ron, washed and hung to dry, then folded and sorted by colour. The small bits are contained in stacked clementine boxes and in baskets hanging from the beams; they are a multitude of colour and texture waiting to be chosen for the next rug. The way I've organized the array of colours on the shelves gives me the ability to pick and choose from what I see in front of me. I'm so lucky to have a studio that works so well for me.

Unfortunately, the open boxes of wool attract moths. People have different ideas about how to get rid of moths, but my solution is to douse the woolen material up and down in a sink of hot, soapy water, rinse thoroughly, and hang dripping wet on the clothesline to dry. You can watch a moth instantly die when it hits soapy water, and the eggs go down the drain with the water. Hanging the fabric without wringing it dry results in nice flat fabric to store away until needed.

I did this to all the wool in all those little boxes three times over. Last year I invested in totes from the department store, and that will keep the moths away, but the pretty coloured wools are hiding away in plastic storage. I miss my little boxes!

The Kedy Place

54" × 27"
Hand-dyed and recycled wool and one-ply
hand-spun yarn on linen, #5 cut
2000

Chosen as one of the best
hooked rugs submitted to
A Celebration of Hand-Hooked Rugs.

In the summer of 2000, Morrey Ewing and Sharon Barrett-Ewing asked if I would consider hooking a rug for them.

I avoid commissions. When someone asks me to do a piece for them I find it difficult to imagine what they see in their minds as the finished product. They always accept my finished piece, but I'm never sure it's exactly what they wanted. That's probably why I prefer making my own images and then selling them to someone who loves what I've created. (I have enough ideas swirling around in my head for two or three lifetimes.)

The Ewings live and work in Toronto, but their hearts are here in Nova Scotia. They own a lovely old property in the nearby community of Mahone Bay known locally as "the Kedy place," and they spend holidays and summer vacations there with their children, Annie and Alexander.

The rug they wanted made was to be a gift for Sharon, and Morrey wanted her to have some input into its design. On Thanksgiving Day of that year I sat around their kitchen table and listened to Sharon talk about her memories of growing up in Nova Scotia, and her love of this very old homestead with its flowers and trees.

There were orange daylilies and a wonderful crabapple tree growing on their property in Mahone Bay. The crabapple tree was beautiful when it was in bloom, but it was also lovely in the fall when it was covered with apples. From the mining town where she lived as child, Sharon remembered white hollyhocks growing in

impossible places, and the gorgeous lupines that grow wild along our roadsides in June. Her eyes shone as she talked and I couldn't help but be inspired to the do the rug she wanted. It was to hang in the living room near the piano and this location determined its dimensions: fifty-four by twenty-seven inches.

The Ewings went back to Toronto and I went to work. Although I don't always enjoy commissioned work,

I loved every minute of this one. I have so much wool on hand from my many years of hooking that I had a multitude of colours to use. But I also did some special dyeing. I used raw sheep's wool and spot-dyed it for the crabapple tree and then dyed some more in soft greens to add interest to the lawn textures.

The fence was a challenge. I drew lines across the linen backing for top and bottom and then started on the

right and hooked two rows of fence, one row of background, two rows fence, one row background all the way across the rug. I think it might have taken longer to hook this fence than if I had actually constructed it with a hammer and nails!

Then I added the path leading into the property and surrounded it with all of Sharon's memories. My interview with her had given me much insight into what she wanted. The property is so beautiful anyway that the rug just galloped along, and it was finished when they came back to Mahone Bay that Christmas.

They picked it up on December 24, and when Sharon saw it, her hands went up through her hair, her eyes shone bright, and she said, "Oh, Doris!" There was a tear in Morrey's eye when he saw how pleased she was, and I knew they weren't just being polite. They really liked it.

My Word

Approximately 42" rounded
All-wool rags, #5 cut, on linen backing
1989

Chosen as one of the best hooked rugs submitted to *A Celebration of Hand-Hooked Rugs*.

This rug is a personal favourite that I thought I would never part with because it was so interesting to make and so many friends shared in it. They gave me "their word."

I have always loved words, and it was an old expression of my grandmother's that inspired the whole concept. She would come indoors on a cold or wet day, hug herself, and say "whimpth the seekability." It seemed to suggest she was drawing in the warmth of the room and I've always been intrigued by it. I have no idea of its origin.

I asked my hooking friends to each give me their word and I would hook it into a mat. Each of us has a favourite word and for many friends, that word burst forth spontaneously. But others wanted to think about it and they came back to our hooking group the next week with their thoughtfully chosen word. It surprised me that no two people chose the same word.

I began with my grandmother's phrase and hooked it into the upper left-hand corner. The words given by my friends suggested the overall design, with "moonlight," "fantasy," "bramble," "mystery," and "enchantment." My husband gave me "faithfulness," the only word hooked in script. "Love," "joy," "peace," and "cozy" are tucked in around the trees. "Halcyon," "contentment," and "tranquility" are caught in its branches.

It was such fun to join the group each week with one or two new words hooked in. Everyone was interested in seeing his or her word added as the rug progressed. The rug came alive then, and took on a form of its own.

"Widdershins" is an English word meaning counterclockwise, or going against the grain. "Abilene" is an obsolete Scottish word meaning the coolness on the underside of the pillow, and "aislin" is an Irish word meaning dream, or vision. "Happy," "freedom," and "musing" are at the base of the scene. "Trek" suggests a long hard journey and "taima" was given to me by a lady who retired from teaching in the Yukon. It is the Inuit word for "The End," so I guess she had the last word.

Each word is meaningful and I remember who submitted it. The whole reminds me of the wonderful friends I have made through this craft called "hooking."

But never say never. I sold this rug to a dear friend who worked with the hearing impaired during much of her career; words meant so much to her.

The Wave

55″ × 27″
Yarn, wool, and fish leather
on linen backing
1990

Chosen as one of the best hooked rugs
submitted to *A Celebration of Hand-
Hooked Rugs.*

A friend and I met one day to go hooking and we pooled our cars at Crescent Beach, a lovely spot on the South Shore of Nova Scotia well known for its unspoiled beauty. There'd been a recent storm and the waves were in turmoil. We watched them crash onto the sandy beach, each wave full of Irish moss that it tossed into the air before pounding it onto the beach and pulling itself back out to sea. It was just a beautiful, sparkling day.

We must carry such images with us without knowing it. Later, when a weaver gave me some thrums that were the very colour of the Irish moss I remembered from that day at Crescent Beach, I knew exactly what I wanted to do with them. I set about creating my own wave.

Another gift of fish leather that had been tanned on nearby Cape Sable Island became the dark little fishes far out at sea. The rug is hooked on a rug warp backing with wool cut to #5 width, and it has a sleeve on the reverse side for hanging. It was not intended to be a rug for the floor.

The dyeing and colouring for the rest of the rug are a whole other story. Dyes come in paper envelopes and when the packages are emptied, there is a powdery residue of colour left in each envelope. I save these empty packets and put similar colours together in a large dye pot. When I have several envelopes, I add lots of water and some vinegar, and then put wool into this simmering mess, pushing the fabric into the colours bleeding from the envelopes. I'm careful not to mix and stir too much. I call this my end-of-package dyeing and it usually gives me the most unusual colours, which I can never achieve in any other way and, of course, can never duplicate.

Another interesting note: The sea moss is used locally as a fertilizer. It is piled for a few months or spread directly on the land and then plowed into the soil when it's time to plant in the spring. Vehicles line up on the beach after a storm and load tubs or plastic bags with this useful gift from the sea. You know it is a good day to harvest Irish moss when you notice droppings all along the road, leaving a trail back to the source, much like Hansel and Gretel with their crumbs of bread.

The fish leather was produced in Clark's Harbour along our South Shore, and was crafted into wallets, jewelry, and other small objects. It cut easily on my cutting machine.

Sea Wrack

52.5″ × 105.5″
Wool / wool yarn, #5 cut on linen backing
1993
Chosen as one of the best hooked rugs submitted to *A Celebration of Hand-Hooked Rugs*.

The idea for *Sea Wrack* came from a sketch I did many years ago. I came across the sketch again after having been out in a boat and being inspired by what I saw growing on the bottom of the ocean. I paired up the sketch with some new imagery I drew, and *Sea Wrack* was born.

"Wrack" means kelp or seaweed, but it's not a common term. When I was researching some of the seaweeds I wanted to include, I came across a wonderful poem called "Sea Wrack":

The wrack was dark an' shiny
where it floated in the sea
There was no one in the brown boat
but only him an' me;
Him to cut the sea wrack,
me to mind the boat
An' not a word between us the hours
We were afloat.
The wet wrack
The sea wrack
The wrack was strong to cut.
from "Sea Wrack" by Moira O'Neil

This is the largest rug I've ever hooked. I thought I should research the many shapes of what I was hooking, so I took out a library book and carefully copied the proper drawings of the various kelp. When I tried to design the rug from these drawings, it was very tight and stiff-looking, so I put the drawings aside and just drew my design freehand directly onto the linen backing. That gave me the look I was seeking.

I had fun dyeing many yucky seaweed colours. When I ran out of a colour as I was hooking, I simply re-drew the area I was working on to accommodate the colours of wool that were left. One segment in the lower left-hand corner is actually hooked with dried seaweed. The ever-changing design became an absorbing, creative experience. It took me a year to complete this rug, but I didn't care if I ever finished it because it was so enjoyable.

I think almost all the wool in this rug is dyed or over-dyed. The yarn was dyed by the lady who spun it. She spins raw fleece directly on to the wheel and produces a very unique product. The cut of wool fabric is #5 throughout.

Lichened

32" × 36"
Recycled and found woolen material,
#5 cut, on linen backing
2000

Lichened illustrates what I like to do best with nature—zoom in on it and be amazed by what I see when I get really close. The lichen on this rock was just full of colour. I chose to hook this rug in the shape of a rock, as it seemed more organic. Ron didn't think this rug would ever sell, but people came by from Vancouver who were studying lichen, and my rug was just their thing!

People are always interested to learn how long it takes me to hook a rug. So much depends on how much interest I have in the piece. Sometimes I can hardly sleep because I'm thinking about how I want the rug to go, so I get up and hook and hook and hook. And before you know it, I've got a whole section done.

"Lichened" was a rug like that. I was just fascinated with its textures and colours, and it probably took me about a month to complete. I hooked it using a #5 cut, my favourite cut for a while as it gave me a little more freedom to achieve the detail, but is quite fine looking overall.

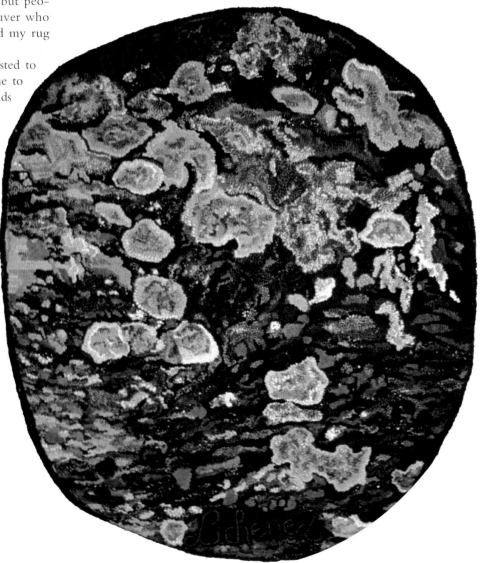

O, Fish of the Sea

54″ × 48″
Recycled and over-dyed woolen fabric,
#6 cut, on burlap
1988
In the permanent collection of the Nova
Scotia Designer Crafts Council

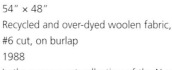

This rug was originally hooked for an exhibition entitled "Fish," sponsored by the Lunenburg County Arts Council of Nova Scotia in 1988. The title of the exhibition reminded me of a fairy tale written by the Brothers Grimm, which I'd often heard as a child. It is the story of a poor fisherman who caught a wonderful fish that granted him his every wish. His greedy wife asked for more and more, but the fish could not grant her the power to rule the rising of the sun and moon, so it returned the humble fisherman and his wife to the poor hovel where they began, and where they live to this day.

This rug was hooked in what I consider the true tradition of this craft. I used old fabrics, in plains and tweeds, and dyed wool from my extensive ragbag, all cut into wide strips (#7 cut) and hooked with a large hook onto a burlap backing. The black outline I've used is frowned on today by modern rug hookers, but it was commonly used in my grandmother's time. I think it lends its own special effect to hooked rugs.

In The Beginning

31″ × 47″
New and recycled wool fabric, #6 cut, on burlap
1968

This began as a design for a fence panel surrounding the construction site of Scotia Square Mall in Halifax in the late 1960s. All the building rubble was on the ground, and the contractor erected a large fence to surround it, using four-by-eight-foot sheets of plywood, then invited artists from all over Nova Scotia to paint a panel. When I came home from painting mine, I thought, "There's a rug in that."

This rug is quite different from my other pieces. It's reminiscent of the rugs I did using aboriginal and Navajo themes. It depicts mountains and valleys, lakes and rivers, trees and sky, much as I would imagine the earth to be "in the beginning." I used "found" material for this rug, which means it's recycled but it's "as is"—old wool blankets, for example, not over-dyed and without much texture, in colours of rust, black, greens, and whites.

When I started hooking this rug I used new white materials that I wanted to cut into wide strips, but the fabric was so heavy and stiff that the loops looked very unattractive from the top. From the underside, though, they were very neat. So I just turned my pattern over when I wanted to fill in the white areas and hooked from the reverse side. I liked the three-dimensional effect so much that I used it purposely for the rest of this rug.

A Periwinkle in an Oyster Bed ▼

60" × 24"
Recycled and found wool fabric, #5 and
#6 cut, on linen
2000

Tall Trees and Hollyhocks ▶

30" × 36"
Found wools, roving, using a variety of
cuts, on linen backing
2008

I thought it was a neat idea to hook an oyster bed. I had hooked a rug of a very large oyster one year earlier and I had a whole collection of shells sitting in a basket. First I tried arranging them on my drafting table but they always looked too posed, so I just tumbled them out onto the floor and out with them came a little periwinkle. And there was my rug design, of a periwinkle in an oyster bed.

A man bought this rug for his wife as a gift for a special occasion. She put it beside her bed and any of her grandchildren who were five feet tall or less could have a nap in the oyster bed. I thought that was neat, and it means the right people got that rug. Imagine sleeping in an oyster bed!

A Periwinkle in an Oyster Bed was never exhibited. It was purchased here at my studio on a Studio Rally week-end, when artists all over Nova Scotia open up their studios to the public.

My husband, Ron, and I were in the Annapolis Valley, celebrating our anniversary. We were just roaming around an antique shop with a carriage house out back that was full of more antiques, and my eye was caught by a stand of hollyhocks growing nearby. There was nothing holding them up, they were just growing there, freestanding, and there were so many colours.

I took a few pictures of them and when I was next looking for inspiration for a rug, there it was! The trees behind the hollyhocks were very tall, and the light was coming through in such a lovely way that it was a perfect image for me.

I used this rug recently at a rug-hooking symposium to demonstrate how simple it can be to put a pattern on a backing. For this rug, all I did was draw a little space where the light was coming through the trees. I drew a few branches, then I shaded in the darkness under the hollyhocks, and made the lines to illustrate the way the hollyhocks were growing. And that was all I had on my backing when I started this rug. So this was a case of the hooking making the picture, and it's a good example of what I call an impressionistic style of rug hooking.

"Tall Trees & Hollyhocks"

~Doris Eaton~ 2008

Reford Gardens

47" × 31"
Hand-dyed new wool and found wool,
#3 cut, on linen
2001

When our friends and neighbours Stephanie and Robert Reford wished for a tapestry hooked of the beautiful Reford Gardens in Quebec, I agreed to do it although I'd never seen the actual gardens. Alexander, the director of the gardens, sent me many pictures and articles, enough to inspire me. The dimensions were to be 47" × 31" and the gardens were quite complicated, requiring a #3 cut. When it was finished the Refords were delighted with it.

The Reford Gardens are the extraordinary achievement of Elsie Reford, a passionate gardener and our friend Robert's grandmother. Elsie had inherited her uncle's fishing camp on the Metis River in Quebec, 220 miles northeast of Quebec City.

In 1926 at the age of fifty-four, she began transforming the camp into a garden, and over the next three decades she designed and created the northernmost public gardens in the eastern half of North America. Known as Les Jardins de Métis, and to others as the Reford Gardens, they have become quite famous since they were first opened to the public in 1962.

Today the gardens are renowned for their exceptional collections and historic plantings, featuring over three thousand species of both native and exotic plants. Where others failed, Elsie Reford somehow succeeded in cultivating rare plants that she imported from around the world. The gardens remain open to the public and are preserved by a team of gardeners and staff.

At the same time I was hooking my Reford Gardens rug, Robert Reford had been asked to write a booklet about his memories of the garden when he visited it as a child, to coincide with the seventy-fifth anniversary celebrations to be held at

the garden in early July. His book was published, as well as a CD.

My tapestry was just finished as the search began for suitable cover artwork for both, so my rug was chosen. The Refords were invited by the Lieutenant-Governor of Quebec to a concert at the gardens. Ron and I were also invited, and we had a wonderful trip.

I hadn't seen the gardens when I hooked the tapestry, but Robert said, "You won't believe how close you've come to what it looks like." And he was delighted that I had hooked his grandmother into the garden path.

Lunenburg Bumps

44" × 20"
Woolen fabric hand-dyed for authentic
house colours
1992

A "bump" is a fascinating archi-tectural feature found on some of the houses in Lunenburg. A bump held a big window at its top, which I think was used by women to watch out over the harbour to see when the ships were coming back from fishing.

For this rug I chose four houses with bumps, took pictures of them, lined them up in a row, and then hooked them for an exhibit at the Black Duck Gallery in Lunenburg.

The man who purchased this rug owned the red house, called Ashley House.

Raindrops on Seaweed

33″ × 27″
Hand-spun and recycled wool, #6 cut, on linen backing
2004

I had taken a photo from above the water, looking down into the seaweed, but it was out of focus. That blurry look gave me the idea for composing this piece around the breaking of the surface of the water. To achieve the sense of depth, of looking down, I used light colours in the foreground with deeper values in the background. I was pleased with the abstract quality the poorly focused photo gave the finished rug.

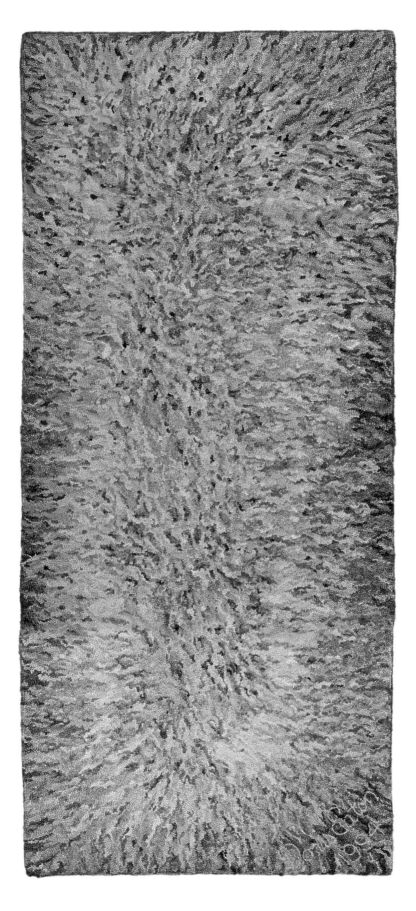

Monet's Garden

48″ × 112″
100% wool spun from Doris's own sheep,
hand-dyed
1994

---

*M*onet's Garden is huge. It's been tromped on in my house by three people and a dog since 1994. Nobody takes their shoes off in my house, and this rug doesn't look much different now than when I hooked it.

I hand-dyed the wool from our own sheep. I saved their fleece every year when we sheared them, and it was a massive job washing it at the end of a few years. Raw wool is very dirty and needs a lot of washing. But I found a nearby sheep farmer who could spin it for me into one-ply yarn that was perfect, about the size of my little finger. It had a twist in it, and that's probably why it's worn so well all these years. That wool just drank up the dye!

My idea was to create an impressionistic garden, a rug with lots of colours, greens and pretty reds. A very light background contributes to the desired soft effect.

My Friendly Garden #1

30″ × 53″
New wool, hand-dyed, #4 cut, on cotton
rug warp
1988

---

*M*y *Friendly Garden #1* was a very interesting rug to hook. I had become fascinated by the "zapping" of images on the TV into small squares of colour—I learned it was called "pixelated." I wanted to try hooking that effect into a rug and I chose to interpret a watercolour that I'd painted of my garden.

I used rug warp for the backing material because its weave is so perfectly even, both horizontally and vertically. Of course it was impossible to simply draw my watercolour design directly onto the backing. It took me almost two hours to draw a grid onto the backing, and then I drew two lines across the surface to indicate the top and the bottom of the fence—that's all.

The first form I began with was the quince tree. Using greys and browns, I started hooking the trunk, worked my way up and out along the branches until I was pleased with the general shape of the tree. Then I added leaves in many shades of green.

Next I hooked mounds of delphiniums and sunflowers because they were in front of the fence in my original watercolour. Along with the flowers I started to suggest the stone path that leads into the picture. Then I hooked the fence in whites with grey for shadows, to give it contour; added the suggestion of trees and shrubs in the distance behind the fence; and finally put in all the lovely blues and mauves of the sky.

The entire rug is hooked back and forth in the small squares: four rows in each square, four stitches in each row. As I hooked back and forth, my stitch twisted when I backed up. This isn't apparent on the front, but on the reverse side it made for an interesting overall pattern.

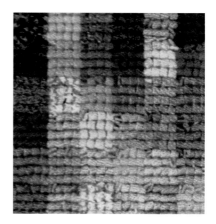

It wasn't easy to hook so closely on a piece which was only recognizable from some distance. The image was all in my mind's eye, so I had to concentrate on the overall effect I wanted for *My Friendly Garden*. But a camera makes all the difference to the viewer. The camera's eye captures exactly what I'd hoped to do, better than the real thing.

Family Saph Rug

112″ × 40″
All new hand-dyed wool fabric, #3 cut, on
100% cotton rug warp
1987

A saph rug is a communal prayer rug, really a series of prayer rugs that, in Muslim tradition, are used only by men. But I wanted mine to be a family rug. I designed a plain mihrab, or centre, that was identical for each of our five children, and then planned a grid for the spandrels, or corners, that I interpreted vertically, horizontally, or diagonally at the top of each arch.

The mihrab in a mosque is an architectural niche built into the wall to indicate the direction of Mecca. The prayer rug provides the Muslim with a miniature temple for his prayer and so the shape includes an arch, pointed toward Mecca. A Muslim would kneel on the centre field and place his hands in the upper corners of the spandrel and his forehead on a centre jewel, often a turquoise.

I have not attempted to be authentic in representing a true prayer rug, but I had fun with the symbolism and incorporated it to make an interesting story for my own family rug.

Another symbol is a "cloud band" and there are a few suggested, but I have also introduced a "wave band" around the base area to suggest the water all around us here in Nova Scotia. The section below each mihrab is different in each rug and tells a personal story of each of my family members.

Starting with our oldest daughter in the panel to the left, this area tells us that P (Patricia) married E (Earl) in 1972. It also indicates that they have one daughter, quite independently off by herself in a soapbox derby car that she raced every year when she was growing up. In their early married life they lived in Hamilton, Ontario, but Earl was transferred to Nova Scotia after his first visit with us.

I had interviewed each of our children about what they wanted me to include in this rug, and my daughter Patricia wanted daisies, which I placed at the top where the hands would rest in prayer. The cross in the centre of the arch represents the Roman Catholic Church that has become her faith.

In the second panel I hooked a comb at the top of the arch and within the wave band, because my daughter's husband has a beard and the comb would remind him to groom

The running dog, another traditional symbol, is held in check by their daughter. A comb is depicted at the top of the arch in their panel because Doug has a beard. The upper corners suggest wheels because the whole family revolves around wheels—from trains, to bicycles, a car, a Jeep, an antique car, and motorcycles, which are Doug's interest.

Because my daughter JoAnn married a fisherman, ship's wheels are at the upper corners and a lamp hangs at the top of her mihrab. Within her wave band we learn that J (JoAnn) married G (Gerald) in 1978 and that their three boys are buddies, so they are close together in their space. Their home, surrounded by trees, is to one side and fish, their livelihood, are on the other.

When I hooked this saph rug, Bradford, our youngest, was not married. His interest in hunting is suggested at the bottom of his panel. The hammer at the top suggests he hammered out a life for himself, and the stereo speakers in the corners are included because of his interest in music.

The border around each panel is a vine that flows without beginning or end, symbolically binding our family together. The half-size end panels suggest my husband and me; the grid includes all the colours used in the rug, suggesting that our children draw from each of us in the pattern of their lives.

Along the top of the entire rug are the names of our children and their mates, and the dates of their birth over the pertinent panels. Along the bottom edge are their children and their birthdates for a complete family record. Ron and I were married on September 10, 1950, and the rug was completed in 1987, after seven years of work.

The colours in this rug certainly are not traditional; they are my personal choice. The rug began with the centre panel. Once those colours were established, it was most difficult to find colours that worked well with them and still provided some contrast. The next panel suggested blues because of the theme of fishing, with water in mind. Once that was worked out, it was necessary to balance it with similar colours on the other side of the centre panel. Then the first and fifth panels picked up colours harmonizing with the centre panel. All the colours for the end panels for my husband and I came from the basket beside my feet. It was fun to pick out the coloured strips at random and hook them in. Besides, I was on the last lap of a very long project and it went along quite quickly from then on.

The all-wool fabric from new and used materials was hand-dyed and cut with the finest blade of my cutting machine. Except for the outlines, the entire rug was hooked horizontally to simulate the original rugs from the Orient that were knotted or woven in straight rows across the whole width of the rug.

This is truly a heritage piece, and I hope my family will enjoy it for generations to come. I feel good about creating something that will last beyond my time and place.

for prayer. D (Donna) married R (Richard) in 1972 and Donna wanted black tulips worked into her design, which incidentally, is an important motif of the tulip period during the reign of Ahmed III (1703–30). Donna and Richard's three daughters are growing between the tulips.

The third panel is of M (Mary) who married D (Douglas) in 1975. Of the two boys in their family, one was obsessed with trains when he was a child, and because I didn't want to include a locomotive, I designated a camel to suggest a "camel train."

JAPAN AND BRIDGEWATER

In August 2001 I received an invitation from Fumiyo Hachisuka of Tokyo to exhibit rugs at an autumn exhibition of her students' work in Japan. I had met Fumiyo at the first meeting of the International Rug Hooking Guild held at Oak Island Inn in Nova Scotia. She is a single mother raising two daughters by teaching rug hooking to Japanese women at cultural centres.

I made many phone calls and followed many leads but I couldn't find a way to insure my rugs for transport to Japan. I mentioned my dilemma at the next meeting of my hooking friends. "Well," they said, "your rugs should go—and you must take them! And Jan (Moir), you go with her and make sure she comes home again."

But this seemed impossible—I had no passport. But Myra spoke up—she was authorized to take passport photos and someone else knew how I could get a passport in a hurry. But how would I submit photos and descriptions of my rugs, authorized and stamped by the immigration department in Halifax? No problem, another friend said. Tickets? Expensive, but I might qualify for a Canada Council grant to cover travelling expenses to install artworks in a foreign country.

Every hurdle I threw at my hooking group, they had an answer for. I went home with my head in the clouds and told Ron. "Well," he said, "I don't know…" But Jan went home and told her husband, Jim, that it was all set—she was going to accompany me to Japan!

When Ron heard there was someone to go with me, all systems were go. My friend Jan Moir is an experienced traveler, and I don't think I could have done it without her. In my wildest dreams I never would have imagined a trip to Japan. Our ten days there were such an adventure, and I still can't believe we did it.

One thing in particular created a lasting impression. When Japanese people bow to each other, it is truly done with deep respect. I'm not suggesting we imitate their gesture, but only that we can apply this feeling of respect in the groups we belong to. It has everything to do with the way we treat each other. It's what makes our hooking groups the treasures they have become for us all.

I hooked a memory of our trip, called "Tokyo," and my hooking friends loved it. You'll hardly believe what they did next. I hadn't been successful in getting a grant from the Canada Council to cover my travel, so these friends commissioned me to hook a special piece for the Des-Brisay Museum in Bridgewater. And this commission paid for my trip to Japan! That meant so much more to me than getting a government grant.

Japan ▼

17" × 46"
Silk, hand-dyed new wool fabric, and recycled wool on linen backing
The foreground is a #5 cut, mid-ground a #4, and background is #3
2003

I was in Japan in the fall and started this rug shortly after I got home. It almost hooked itself—I had brought home images from Japan for inspiration, but I just seemed to know what this rug should look like. The idea for dividing the rug into panels was inspired by an art exhibit I saw in Japan, where the panels were vertical screens traditional to Japanese culture. I used that idea, but made my panels horizontal instead.

At the bottom of the rug is the word Tokyo, hooked using one of the simpler dialects of Japanese. To the right of that is an image of little

sake cups. The image of the bird of prey sitting on the branch is from an incredible painting by a well-known Japanese artist. The next image up, the second panel from the bottom, depicts the fishing industry. I created that image directly from a postcard. The third panel up is a shrine we saw in a Shinto temple. George Bush had been talking war at that time, and the Japanese people remain very conscious about war, so the Shinto temple had been open for a whole month for people to pray for peace. The little figures directly in front of the temple were hooked with the silk from a kimono that belonged to my friend Fumiyo's grandmother. I've also depicted a large urn that was constantly smoking. People would gather around it and waft that smoke toward them as a healing process.

The next panel up shows a whole long row of persimmon trees, the fruit of which we had every morning for breakfast. They look just like apple trees. The panel above that depicts a shrine to a well-known artist of a few centuries ago, Gyokudo Kawai, whose property has been made into a museum; it's like a resort or a vacation spot, where you can see his work. A river runs by this property, and we had a picnic that Fumiyo put together for us. We saw Japanese men put their kayaks in the river and ride the rapids. Almost all of them lost their kayaks along the way, and there were people at the bottom in a pool picking the kayaks out of the water. It was the end of October and a few of the trees had colour. The weather was perfect.

Of course, the very top panel is Mount Fuji, which we saw from a distance on our travels. Our other Japanese friend Fumiko, whom we stayed with for three days, took us on a two-and-a-half-hour train trip north of Tokyo into mountainous country. We looked back toward Tokyo, and there was Mount Fuji, highest and most beautiful of all the mountains.

Bridgewater

18″ × 53″
Hand-dyed, over-dyed recycled wool fabric
on linen backing
2003

When I told the DesBrisay Museum that my hooking friends had commissioned me to hook a rug for the museum, the staff gave me some images that I ended up using in my pattern. It became a different style of rug for me, because I don't hook figures very often.

The top panel is a winter scene north of Bridgewater, and the second panel is the carding mill run by the museum. The narrow panel below that is the new Veterans Bridge in Bridgewater that goes across the LaHave River. The panel below that depicts the museum itself. The bottom panel is a couple wandering through the beautiful grounds behind the museum, where there's a duck pond surrounded by lovely trees and open spaces.

Tranquility

17" × 30"
Woolens, rovings, skein of coarse yarn,
hooked on a linen foundation material
2007

I began *Tranquility* with a river running through at the bottom. But I just couldn't get the rest of the rug to go with it—nothing would work. I would hook something in and then take it out, over and over again. Sometimes it's very hard to know how something is going to look *until* you hook it in.

Finally I put in long tree trunks, some narrow, some wide, rising up to the sky, but I had no idea what I was going to do in between. Then I went back to my stripey rugs and found that if I put stripes in horizontally and created a landscape that way, it became a walk through the trees.

This design was hard work. I was lost in it and didn't know where I was going. I was using recycled wool and yarn that was black and blue and very coarse, like horsehair. It was perfect for the trees. I am getting very interested in texture, more and more all the time as I work at my craft and my art.

I thought I would call this piece "Lost in the Woods," but when it was finished and hanging before me I felt quiet and peaceful. Tranquil.

◀ The Dress

40″ × 108″
1987

This rug is nine feet long and was meant to be a runner in my studio. But when I put the rug down, I couldn't walk on "her."

A lady from New Jersey bought *The Dress* and hung "her" in a stairway under a skylight. The rug even went to England to live for a few years!

Tannery Hollow Lodge ▼

72″ × 36″
Recycled wool, raw sheep's wool
1991

My husband Ron and I ran a bed and breakfast in Petite Rivière, Nova Scotia, for six years and I hooked this rug for the front foyer, to welcome guests and tell them a story.

We named our place Tannery Hollow Lodge, and I wanted the flower border on my rug to suggest the hollow where the house was situated. There were tall trees along our driveway, and it seemed we always had sheets on the line to dry. A brook babbled along by our back door and ducks swam in nearby water. Our vegetable garden and fruit trees supplied food for ourselves and a local canteen at Green Bay. Our cow gave milk and cream and butter, and our chickens supplied eggs. The turkeys and pigs were raised for their meat.

I hooked our sheep with their own wool, which I snipped from their backsides as they grazed in the pasture. As I hooked with the sheep's wool, a deceased tick fell out, and I tucked it into a loop. I'm sure it isn't still there!

Telling a story is a favourite topic for any rug hooker.

◀ Skylark

17″ × 45″
Recycled and found wool materials on linen backing
2002

Skylark is a depiction of the images I see when I look up to the sky. There's a row of moons, there are cloud formations, streaks across the sky, little stars or suns that are going up, up, and away, and at the very top there's a shape similar to a bird, which I called a lark.

At the bottom of the rug there's a stone wall with some plants. But primarily, *Skylark* is a study of the horizon, with cloud formations above it and streaks in those clouds.

Rocky Mountain Road ▼

32″ × 29″
2009

Our daughter JoAnn and her family moved to Edmonton, and after nine years Ron and I went west to visit them.

The Rocky Mountains are so overwhelming; a trip to Banff and Jasper through the mountain ranges proved unforgettable. One photo in particular was so simple and yet captured so much, that I used it to commemorate our trip with this rug.

It is a simple rug, but one of my favourites.

Trek

24″ × 40″
2005

During the 1960s I was involved with large abstract oil paintings. Professor Ian James of the Acadia University Art Gallery in Wolfville had come to our nearby village of Canning and taught several of us in the area to express ourselves with large paintings of wonderful textures and colour. We exhibited our work locally, at various galleries in Halifax, at the Beaverbrook Gallery in Fredericton, New Brunswick, and in Newfoundland. Canada's centennial year, 1967, was a particularly bountiful year for art exhibits.

Some of the large paintings I did at that time became adaptable to the colours and textures of rug hooking, and "Trek" is one such adaptation. I remember my original design was based on thoughts of a very steep precipice and the challenge it posed to mountain climbers with its steep trails and overhanging mists.

How fitting that this rug was purchased by a couple with intense passion for outdoor adventure.

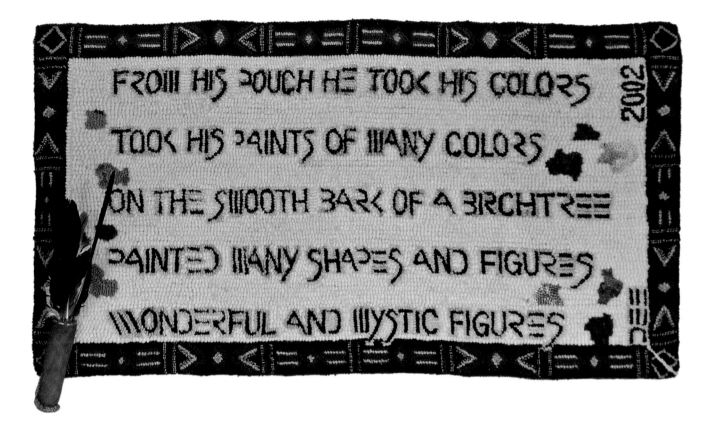

Hiawatha

33" × 17"
Pencil roving background and a variety of
wools
2002

This piece came about after a discussion at a hook-in on lettering. Was it difficult? How do we go about it? The discussion started with signing a rug as it was being finished, with a signature and date, which I feel is very important to every creation we do. One way to become more comfortable with hooking words on a rug is to design your rug using a quote or favourite saying.

Not everyone in our group participated, but some very interesting rugs came of that discussion. My own was a quote from the poem "Hiawatha," by Henry Wadsworth Longfellow. I redesigned the letters, leaving off their vertical lines, and I used pencil roving for the background material. "Pencil roving" is a very thin strand of roving, unspun and thinner than a pencil. It is too thin and weak to hook one strand at a time, so I double the strand, or triple it, to hook it into my work. It is 100 percent wool, of course, and just drinks up the dye. It makes a very fine background.

A dear friend saw this and had to have it, so I see it every time I drop by her house for a cup of tea.

Harvest Time

33.5″ × 25″
1995

When our family lived in the Annapolis Valley, we had apple orchards that were beautiful when they blossomed in the spring. But they were equally interesting at harvest time when the trees were laden with lush red or golden apples, ready for picking.

The background of this rug was hooked from a beautiful Scottish woolen coat given to me by a friend. It just cried out to be hooked into a mat, and the colours made a lively backdrop for the trees and their branches, the bright fruit, and the apple barrel below.

Poppy Tapestry

46" × 32"
1990

I had designed a cross-stitch sampler of our family and I liked the effect of the stitches—up and down, back and forth, no corners. I thought taking that concept and adapting it to hooking and using wool with a wide cut would make a very interesting "tapestry."

I searched for weeks, looking for an image that I could hook this way, and found it in a birthday card I had saved (you just never know!). I started with the poppies, the centre of interest, hooking them in bright colours, then added leaves, and brought it together with the shapes and colours of the Japanese lanterns. The background was hooked in the same style and I was thinking of barnboards as I hooked it. Finally, not rounding the corners and following the weave of the foundation fabric gave me the effect I was looking for. Its style is reminiscent of a cross-stitch picture.

Petite Rivière ▼

38″ × 27″
2010

Skyline ▶

22″ × 36″
2007

I hooked this rug in February, March, and April of 2010 from a photo our daughter Pat had taken in the fall of a location along the Petite Rivière. It was a commission, my choice of image, for a birthday gift for a friend in Ontario.

There was so much colour, and I thought it was a daunting image to tackle, but I just started in one corner and kept going. It is hooked entirely of woolen bits and roving and recycled fibres.

My grandmother died in 1953, and one of the last bits of her winter coat is hooked in near my signature, as it has been in many pieces.

Skyline represents the view from my studio window with beautiful cloud formations in the sky. On a recent visit to a wool shop I was drawn to the colours in a skein of textured wool. This was certainly not the colouring of the clouds that day, but I wanted to use it. It was shaded and worth a try. The result was an interesting wall hanging, mostly because of the unusual colouring of sky and clouds.

Parameciata

45″ × 45″
2001

This rug was from a whimsical sketch in my journal and I drew it directly onto a linen backing. I find square rugs fit some areas in a home very nicely, and this design worked well in that format.

The real interest for me was in the colours I chose. I put a lot of thought into that aspect of this rug, stacking folded wool and adding or removing colours until I was satisfied with the overall look.

I had no idea for a name for the finished rug, but a friend came up with "parameciata," and it seemed to suit well.

Sandstones

48″ × 24″
1998

I designed this rug from a sketch I had drawn along the Bay of Fundy, at Turner's Brook. The wonderful stones on the beach seemed to have been arranged just for me, and their colours and textures against the sand and water made a fine image in my mind for a rug.

I sat with my sketchbook while my children played on the sandy beach and then found a delightful, shallow waterfall coming down from the North Mountain to the Bay of Fundy. We were there all day long. When I came across this sketch years later, I knew what my next rug would be.

Beachcomber

16″ × 27″
2009

This was a commissioned piece for a very specific space in a home. An affection for the seashore, and some great "texturey" stuff I had on hand came together in this design, and it almost hooked itself. It's of no specific place, but rather from my imagination, and it suited the owner's love of the ocean and that special place on her wall.

My hooking friends know what my "texturey stuff" is, and how much I have, but I should clarify, because it's a special term. Textures in hooked rugs and hangings are most effective when using plaids and tweeds, checks and knit sweaters and scarves— actually, almost any fibres that can be drawn through the backing material with a hook.

Sometimes the fibres can be quite heavy and coarse. I have a large coarse hook for these, and hook the loops with more space between stitches, so that I don't "pack" them in.

The effect of these textures is just what we want sometimes for the extra interest we can give a creation, whether it is realistic or abstract. These fibres are the most treasured "stuff" in my stash of wool.

◀ Embryo

28″ × 41″
2006

Leafing through my journal, I came across a pencil sketch that caught my eye, which I probably drew in my art school days. I have no idea what the original inspiration was, but while I was hooking this rug, I thought of it as an embryo—as the beginning or undeveloped state of something. Again, working out the colours was a challenge and the dark and light areas were important as the design came to its conclusion.

Forest Sunset ▶

20″ × 43″
1999

This is a very simple design of trees and foreground. But the rug's colours and the feeling of being in the woods as the sun is going down make it appealing.

Quest

29" × 49"
2008

This rug was a "quest" for a new hooking without a lot of definition. As I worked on it, in my mind I saw trees and falling leaves against a backdrop of distant mountains with the sky above them. Other people see it as an underwater image and relate it back to my earlier works on tidal pools.

This rug has an interesting foreground and a lot of texture. It became abstracted, but I think it holds together well and I certainly enjoyed working on a piece that I more or less composed as I watched it grow.

Slow Motion

20" × 52"
2010

This rug is all about colour. I usually start a rug at a centre of interest and expand out from that beginning. In this case I started with my selections of coloured fibers. There wasn't a lot of any one colour and I wanted all the colours to span the length of the finished piece, so I spaced each shade more or less at random. Then the challenge was to bring them together to a pleasing whole. It worked for me, and it was a new way to develop a pattern.

MY AUNT DORIS

by Luanne Johnson, 1988

Doris, the artist,
The oldest,
The youngest --
Some see "Grandma"
But I see a girl
Who danced on a log
Who found the dead snake
Who cut her own hair
Who made green, new paths.

She went unafraid
To strange houses
And gardens,
Lending to them
Her scent of rich joy.
"She's moving again,"
Her sister tells me
I hear a sigh somewhere
In my mother's voice.

Her family is calm with her fanciful rugs
Her paintings like photos
Her meals fit for wings.

I see her once in a year
And every year her coloured empire
Is greater—
Her floors and walls are
Laden with her soul.

Her stovetop is bright with
Mysterious flavours,
Flowers in bright jars
Crown every table,
And her own flowers dot her study floor—
Their petals spots of paint
On stems of shredded wool.

TIDAL POOL RUGS: "THERE'S A RUG IN THAT!"

I am fascinated with tidal pools and they have been the inspiration for several of my rugs. The fascination began when our friends Earl and Mary Smith invited Ron and me to visit several of the LaHave Islands with them by boat. These islands are on the South Shore of Nova Scotia, near Rissers Beach Provincial Park.

We stopped for a picnic lunch on one small, uninhabited island called Thrumcap. It has rock formations and ledges, a few windswept spruce trees, stunted grasses with scattered wildflowers and foxberry vines, and the seagulls' "dining room table," where the birds drop sea urchins, mussels, and clams from high overhead to break their shells for feasting. And best of all, Thrumcap has three tidal pools, so deep that they never go dry. Over many years these pools have evolved their own ecosystems—wonderfully busy little worlds. We found brilliant green seaweed, live clams, snails, and various swimming bugs, including one we called the helicopter because of the way it propelled its little legs. I took many photographs and kept returning again and again to Thrumcap to satisfy my fascination with all these underwater images. Earl even made me a glass-bottomed box to break the skin of the water so I could take better deep-sea images with my camera.

I just knew that there was a rug in those underwater images. I drew a lot of the bits I remembered directly onto a linen backing. The shells I drew in the corners hadn't been in the pool, but the design needed something to anchor it down.

Tidal Pool #1

41″ × 42″
#5 cut wool on linen
1996

The small stones in the pool became a border along with the frothiness at the edges of the pool.

The very busyness of my pool became the greatest challenge of the whole project. I came to a slow halt about halfway through, lost in this place where too much was going on. At that point I wasn't sure I'd ever finish it, and put it aside to work on other pieces. The encouragement of my husband and friends got me going again and I put it back on my frame and forged ahead until it was done. I'm glad I did because as things turned out, it became one of my favourite rugs.

The more I became interested in shells and their beautiful patterns and subtle colourings, the more I zoomed in on them and made large rugs around this shell theme.

I made three more rugs using this tidal pool theme, and then branched out and created many different designs around the theme of sea, shells, seaweed, and stone.

The Sea Urchin

20" diameter
Recycled wool, roving, yarns on linen
backing
1997

*T*he *Sea Urchin* is composed of five-section segments and was a real challenge. I used all new white wool and carefully dyed the colours to match those of a special sea urchin shell that I had found on the beach at Cherry Hill. This particular shell was quite unique in its colouring—it hadn't bleached out in the sun as they usually do.

A visitor stopped at my studio and was particularly interested in this rug. He was from Wales and was invited to come to Nova Scotia to study the viability of sea urchins for their world market potential. He pointed out something that I had missed. There is a noticeable shape, larger than the others, at the very centre of the shell, which has to do with the shell's movement and the urchin's ability to use its spines to create crevices in rocks.

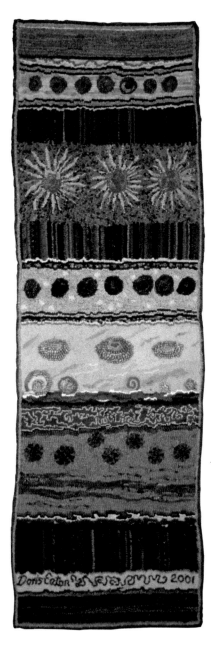

Shore Things ◀

19″ × 65″
Recycled over-dyed wool, textured wool
on linen
2001

This rug is about what goes on down at the seashore. I hooked the wharf with barnacle trails underneath it, a sandy beach with lots of shells, and plenty of sea urchins around.

I was having a lot of fun with texture when I hooked this rug. I found a beautiful old checkered skirt that was just perfect to back up my sea urchins. The stripey wharf came out of one box that was just full of dark colours. This rug was such fun to make.

The Big Oyster ▼

48″ × 48″
Recycled woolen fabric, found wool, over-dyed wool
1999

Ron and I were going to the Celtic Colours music festival in Cape Breton on Thanksgiving weekend and I needed an oyster to pose for my rug design. When I went to the fish counter at Sobeys in Sydney, the gentlemen who waited on me was not taken aback by my request for one "especially handsome" oyster to use for a rug pattern. I remember thinking at the time that someone in his family must hook rugs, too, because the request didn't faze him a bit. He offered to photocopy it for me, but then I wouldn't have the colours I wanted. So he sold it to me for less than a dollar. Ron ate the oyster and I hooked the shell.

Tidal Pool #3

25" × 40"
Recycled wool on linen
2001

After a house fire destroyed our daughter Donna's rugs, she used some of her insurance money to commission a few rugs to replace them.

Her particular request was for her own tidal pool and to my mind this rug—*Tidal Pool #3*—was the most successful of all my tidal pool rugs. It has great colours and the design holds together well. Donna was very pleased with it: *Tidal Pool #3* hangs proudly in her living room.

Sea Strand

20″ × 46″
Recycled wool fabric, roving, yarns on linen
1995

It amazes me that one can become so engrossed with a new rug as it emerges, to the exclusion of all else. *Sea Strand* was such a rug for me. I became fascinated with the total concept.

Like lots of ideas, it turned out differently than I had visualized at the start. My inspiration was the seashore here in Nova Scotia, and I wanted to depict lines in the sand. It took me longer than usual to hook because it took a long time to develop the design in my head, and then translate that through my hands. (Does every rug hooker think a great deal as their piece develops, as I do?)

According to *Webster's Dictionary,* "sea mark" is the line on the coast marking the tidal limit. "Sea strand" simply means seashore, which in turn is officially defined as the ground between the ordinary high water and low water marks. "Strand," in turn, is defined as fibres or filaments twisted, plaited, or laid parallel to form a unit, or "one of the elements interwoven in a complex whole." Since *Sea Strand* conjures up the image of the very fibres we work with in hooking rugs, I had my title.

I studied creative stitches under Jean Gardiner at one of the Nova Scotia rug-hooking schools and found some of those stitches were just right for certain areas of this rug. I used found material and natural one-ply spun wool, and dyed them as I needed them. I left some negative areas unhooked so the natural linen backing became part of the design. The colours in this rug are very limited, as they are when you take a walk along the seashore.

Originally I wanted to integrate actual seaweed into the strands but eventually I removed them because they looked too contrived.

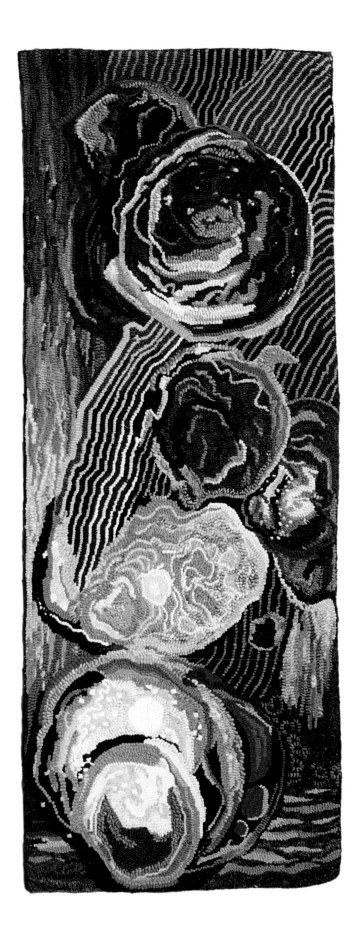

Molluscs

18″ × 47″
Mostly recycled woolen fabric, #5 and #6 cut, on linen
1995

This rug was designed around a fascinating shell that my grandsons gave me. The shell became very frail and broke in two, but I did take a picture of it to illustrate the importance of it in the lower half of the rug amid the oyster and the clam, the bar clam and seaweeds.

This rug was my entry in an exhibition at the Mary E. Black Gallery in Halifax when Nova Scotia celebrated the Year of the Hooked Mat in 1995.

Somethin' Fishy

48″ × 54″
Recycled and found wool, blankets on linen
1999

For many years I've clipped and saved countless images that I think may become inspirations for rugs or colour schemes. These scrapbooks of ideas are invaluable resource materials for me. Several pages in one book are of fish, and when I was designing a rug of swirls and integrating free forms, the graceful shapes and curves of the fish were a perfect match. I could make them twist and flow to follow my design, become the scrolls, and intrude into the centre.

Originally, the fish were to have eyes, fins, and more detail, but they lost a certain rhythm. As a result, I kept them very simple and settled for some texture in a bit of pattern, and made them colourful. The idea was to use up wool from my baskets of scraps from other projects. It was fun and as I developed the rug I decided that for colour, "anything goes."

The centre is hooked contour-style around the fish and scrolls of an off-white wool blanket. The border behind the fish is of dark browns and black, and the khaki seaweeds were from an old army blanket.

This rug was chosen by our daughter Mary, and hangs just inside her front door.

Seaweeds

24" × 36"
Recycled woolen fabric and yarns on linen,
#5 and #6 cuts
2004

This was the final rug of my sea wrack, or seaweed, theme. My stash of colours and dyed pieces left over from years of hooking came out of hiding and this rug just grew into a *very* colourful interpretation. It was purchased by a man who was having trouble with his eyesight and was confined to a wheelchair. He couldn't miss this rug in its spot on the floor.

A Gift from the Sea

36″ × 23″
Carded wool roving, chenile, new and
recycled wool fabric on linen
2007

I designed this rug from a photo I had taken of a boy at nearby Crescent Beach. He had found a special shell and was observing it with fascination. I imagined it might be a moon snail shell and designed it into this piece, adding seaweeds and waves.

The lady who owns the rug was almost moved to tears when she saw it for the first time at an exhibition. It reminded her of her little daughter, who is intensely interested in the things she finds while walking with her grandmother on the miles of beaches near their summer home. Her grandmother is a biologist who shares and encourages the girl's interest. The rug has found a perfect home.

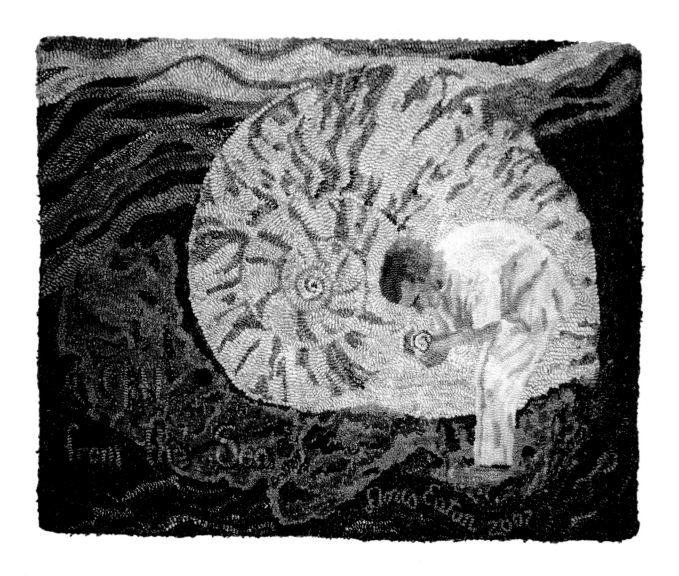

Small Sea Wrack

36″ × 25″
Recycled and found wool on linen
1999

When our daughter Patricia wanted me to hook a rug for her, she requested a smaller version of *Sea Wrack*. This rug hangs in a place of honour and suits her home near the Minas Basin, at the base of Cape Blomidon in the Annapolis Valley of Nova Scotia.

CROW-THEMED RUGS: A PERSONAL FASCINATION

After World War Two my brother was conscripted into the rehabilitation forces sent to Europe, and his young wife, Ginny, and their little son went to live with my mother in Massachusetts. Ginny dubbed Mum "the Old Crow" and gave her a pin that declared Mum a member of the Old Crow Society. Mum enjoyed being an Old Crow, and so my fascination with crows became even stronger.

For a long time, a crow led the way from our driveway almost every time Ron and I took off on a little trip. Once we were visiting Elizabeth Lefort at Margaree in Cape Breton and I burst out to Ron, "Look, there's Mum. She just landed on that tree."

Elizabeth was confused. "What? Your mother?" So I told her I was sure the crow I saw was Mum and that she was accompanying us on this trip.

I designed a sign for my mother's house in Norwood, Massachusetts. It was of a crow sitting on top of the word "Rookery." Our son cut the crow out of wood, I painted it black, and we gave it to Mum for Christmas. She had a "rookery" in Massachusetts and I had a "hookery" in Nova Scotia.

Crowsnest Game Board

12″ × 27″
2008

_____

A nest of crows on a game board. A magnet across the top makes it just right for a fridge magnet. It's now at our daughter Jo's in Edmonton.

Island Trio

26″ × 39″
2010

One time we camped at Murray River on Prince Edward Island next to a spot the crows had chosen for the night. We thought they'd never stop cawing, but darkness finally brought peace and quiet.

Years later, during a short stay on PEI, the crows seemed to be everywhere. I wanted to do a hooking of them; they came to breakfast each day and roosted in an old tree nearby. Our daughter Mary took a picture of them, and for my birthday, Mary gave me her photo and a piece of linen for a new hooking. This is another keeper.

Crowstown ▼

45″ × 45″
2006

A Roost of Crows ▶

43″ × 48″
All recycled wool fabric, #6 cut,
on linen backing
2002

Crows are intelligent birds and very interesting to observe. They also lend themselves very well to rug design, because they are most dramatic with their black feathers and haughty attitudes.

A friend posted a letter to me and addressed it to "Crowstown" rather than the community of Crousetown where I live. Well, there *was* a rug in that!

Crowstown depicts branches and leaves and crows, all hooked to create a heavy, wide border around the sky in the centre.

When the rug was finished the first time, I had hooked a large, round moon in its centre. I put it in an exhibition in Riverport, Nova Scotia, but when I saw the rug hanging on the wall, it was just awful. The moon was too large and all wrong. So when the show was over and the rug came home, I took all of the moon out, re-dyed the wool strips in turquoisey sky colours, mixed it with "texturey" stuff, and re-hooked it into the rug.

A habit of crows is to find a spot to roost for the night. When we lived in the Annapolis Valley in Nova Scotia, our farm was on a point of land reaching out into the Minas Basin. Across from us were the mud flats and headlands of Starr's Point, just outside Wolfville. Before dusk we would see the crows fly in from miles away, coming from north and south, all congregating for the night.

Crows have always fascinated me and I knew there had to be a rug in them. A friend wrote a book called *The Black Spirit* in which he used the term "a roost of crows," and I chose his words to name this rug I did in 2002. It depicts a forest in the centre with crows flying in from every direction. They almost create a border around the perimeter of the rug. There must be some explanation of this habit of crows to come to one central spot at dusk each evening to spend their night together, and then fly off again in the morning.

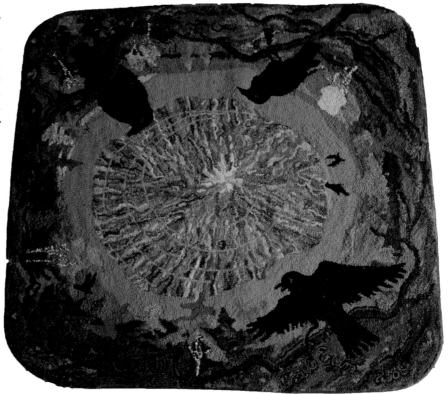

GAME BOARD RUGS: LET'S PLAY!

My game boards are based on traditional wooden ones, and they can be hung on the wall or rolled around dice or checkers and stored in a drawer. I love hooking game boards. The checkerboard pattern is of dark and light squares, so that part is quite simple. But the fun comes in adding the top and bottom segments and I've done many different ones.

I've used my garden for inspiration, and the sea. I've used my sheep and the farm, and in another one I used an abstract painting. The Lunenburg Heritage Society wanted to raise money one year by selling tickets on a hooking, so I made a rug for them that was really popular, with dancing dolphins and a moon in the sky.

Checkerboard Landscape ▼

Parcheesi ▲

Parcheesi boards are fascinating, too. They're a lot of fun because the colour scheme makes all the difference—just the pleasure of putting the colours together and working them out.

My game boards have been well received on studio rally weekends over the years. They're less expensive than a large rug, so when people came to my studio, they could buy a piece of my work without it costing a lot, and there was a practical use for them, too.

Then there are the game board collectors…although this is a new form of game "board," and not really a board at all!

When I finished this "pink" version, I was very disappointed with my colour choice, so I unhooked the pink and replaced it with the blue (Seashells #2) and was satisfied. Friends are so delighted when I have to take things out and re-hook them; I think they can relate to that.

Checkerboard Seashells #2 ▼

Checkerboard Dancing Dolphins

◀ Checkerboard with Oysters
and Five Starfish

Checkerboard Blue Rocks ▼

RUGS USING OUTLINES: BEYOND THE OUTLINE

Using black lines around motifs, as my grandmother did when hooking rugs, has always interested me. Many Nova Scotian rugs were hooked this way in the past so I feel I'm upholding that older tradition when I use outlines in some of mine. Sometimes I almost "see" black lines around objects; this happens in my watercolour painting, too. In painting, the black lines outline my brush strokes and seem to abstract the image and bring it forward in the picture plane.

Cactus Zinnias

44″ × 30″

1998

Chosen by *Rug Hooking Magazine* in 2000.

I love watercolour painting, but rug hooking is my passion. *Cactus Zinnias* was my first attempt to use one of my watercolour paintings as the pattern for a hooked picture.

I enlarged my watercolour painting to the size I wanted and outlined the images. The original painting had several more flowers in it, but when I hooked these into my piece, I didn't like the effect. It was too busy. I took some flowers out and re-hooked the empty shapes in background colours, and they became little "ghost flowers" in the background.

I had been given some raw, unspun sheep's wool in gorgeous colours from a wonderful little store in Pictou, Nova Scotia. I used my newfound wool in combination with plain and textured fabric and with a handspun, one-ply wool that I often use in my work.

The flowers and leaves in "Cactus Zinnias" were wonderful to work on, but the subtleties in the background were the real challenge. And that's the part that everyone loves best.

This rug has been published in *A Celebration of Hand-hooked Rugs*. The rug still hangs in my living room. It's another keeper. I just couldn't part with it.

Treetops and Fireflies

31″ × 40″
2008

The inspiration for this rug came one winter day when I was looking out over our woods. I was amazed at how all those trees appeared as a series of little branches up against the sky. It was such a confusion of branches that I couldn't follow one tree from ground to sky and the resulting maze of silhouettes was fascinating.

When I drew my pattern for this rug I didn't pay any attention to the tree trunks or how the trees were formed, I just let it all be mixed up, as I saw it. I had fun, using my black outlines to edge many dark, rich colours. At the bottom of this rug I wanted a misty, steamy quality to represent the snow in the foreground. I had a brand new toy, a drum carder, so I mixed the white sheep's wool together with the purples and greys of the dark colours of roving, and put them all through my carder at the same time, again and again until they blended into the colours I wanted. I didn't dye any wool, I just carded the wool together until I got my colours. It gave me snow in the foreground, and depth in the woods. I love this technique of using the drum carder to blend colours; I want to experiment with it more in the future.

The fireflies were an accident. I must have had something else on my backing and when I came to this little yellow spot, I thought "Well, I'll just outline it and put more little yellow spots in it too, and call them fireflies." It's fun to go along with these "accidents." To my mind, that's a creative attitude, and can make a difference.

The Red Trillium

30" × 44"
Recycled woolen fabric, #5 cut,
on linen backing
2000

This design was first a watercolour I painted when Ron and I lived in Canning in the Annapolis Valley of Nova Scotia. On the first day of fishing season every spring Ron would take our children, and sometimes the neighbours' children too, and we would all go up over the North Mountain to fish. I didn't do much fishing, but I did take my sketchbook and once I saw a rare red trillium near the brook where we ate lunch. I sat and sketched the red trillium, and did a quick watercolour painting of the image when we came home.

Years later I was looking for inspiration for a new rug and I came across this small watercolour painting. I enlarged the scene and started hooking black outlines to match the painting. I kept to a very restricted palette of colour, using some contrast for the background trees. The red trillium stands out so well and yet blends in easily with its surroundings.

Concentrating on subtle colouring in the trees and then adding the red flower was challenging. This is another rug I can't part with; it hangs on our living room wall at home.

Little Green Apple

36″ × 36″
1992

My husband and I were on the board of the Folk Art Society of Nova Scotia at one time. I was fond of the simple, honest works of art by craftspeople who had no formal art training. In keeping with this, I designed *Little Green Apple*, just for fun, trying to keep it simple in the folk art style.

Stripey Rugs: "Endless Creative Possibilities"

Stripes have always been a favourite theme in fabrics and fibre art. I have my own interpretation of stripes and I find they are a pleasure to design and to hook, because they offer endless creative possibilities.

I start with my linen cut to the size I want for the mat. Starting at the top, I draw lines with a felt-tip marker directly onto the backing. I want the lines to be vertical so they go from top to bottom, but in a very random fashion. I have no idea where they're going—if they bump into each other, I go back up to the top again and start a new line. Soon a pattern emerges. It's fascinating! Nothing is planned at the beginning; the lines just make their own pattern. I feel sometimes as though there's a divine hand leading me on.

The real fun begins when I choose the colours and hook them in, row by row, colour by colour. Mostly I use contrasting colours next to each other, to develop the overall effect I want. But sometimes I outline these lines with a thin strand of colour, maybe black or wine or navy, to achieve a different look.

Striptease

33" × 40"
2003

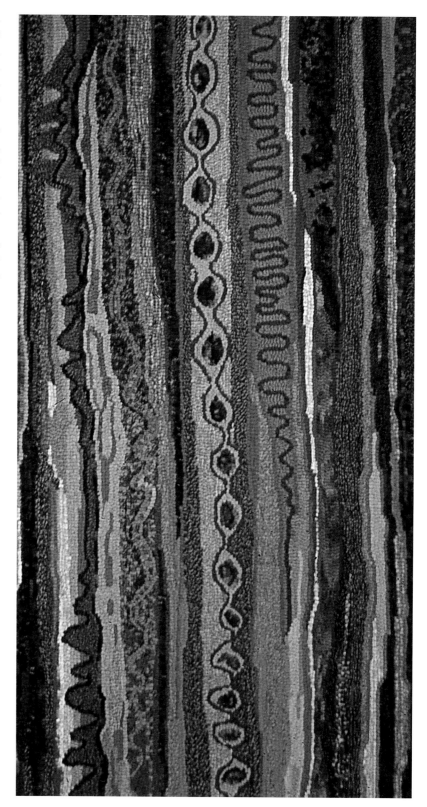

My first intentional stripey rug was created as a release from being housebound one winter, after some very bad snowfalls. A friend had given me her woven "bits," which she had rolled up by colour. So I would unroll one and put that colour in, and then unroll another and put that in. The colours looked good together and I called this rug *Striptease*.

Stripes (January rug)

28″ × 52″
2005

My second stripey rug was called "January" and was bright and colourful to offset the continual stormy weather and cancelled hook-ins that winter.

Stripes (March rug) ▼

54″ × 29″
2005

The third in this series was another response to miserable weather. It became my favourite because of its subtle blues and greens and a hint of trees and sky in the design. By then I was ready for spring, so I named this one "March."

I had a lot of fun with these stripey rugs because I could do anything I wanted. But you know, if someone asked me to design one of these today, I'd find it hard to do. It's a phase I went through. I did stripey rugs all that year and now it's hard to go back and do another one.

The next progression was to combine stripes with other elements of design. A few examples of these are *Iris Trio*, *Spring Thaw*, *Tranquility*, *Myra*, and a horizontally striped landscape, *Kingsport Trees*.

Silver Threads Among the Gold

23″ × 31″
2005

This rug was hooked for Art Hits the Wall, an exhibition at the Rossignol Cultural Centre in Liverpool in 2005, and the chosen theme was an interpretation of a song or poem. I chose the song "Silver Threads Among the Gold" and hooked an imaginative head of hair. Why? Because it applied—to me:

"Darling, I am growing old.
Silver threads among the gold."

◀ Spring Thaw

50" × 29"
2008

Spring Thaw became a horizontally striped landscape of the endless freezing and thaw of a long spring season in 2008. Various textures made it an interesting piece to hook, matching the texture to lands and fields, sky and grasses.

Kingsport Tree ▼

37" × 17"
2003

Kingsport Tree suggests a horizontal landscape with a line on the distant headland, where our farm was located in the Annapolis Valley. Landscapes certainly lend themselves to a horizontal theme.

The old tree as you drive into Kingsport has been there as long as I can remember, and is now beginning to show its age. The marshlands and distant Minas Basin are always precious scenes to me.

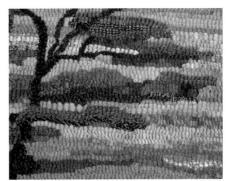

◀ Myra

17.5″ × 30″
2010

This rug was a commission for a dear friend, and uses the stripey background with hollyhocks, and forget-me-nots in the foreground so she won't forget me!

Iris Trio ▶

31″ × 44″
2004

Iris Trio is a design I created for a smaller piece with a plain background, but enlarging the flowers and providing a woodsy, stripey background gave them a much more interesting setting that was just what the design needed.

ABORIGINAL DESIGN RUGS:
ABORIGINAL INSPIRATIONS

I've always had a fascination with Native designs. I find them to be pure and true, both traditional and modern at the same time. Their colours lend themselves to modern decor and when they hang in any room, they become its focal point.

Glooscap

74″ × 36″
1963

This is the first rug I ever designed and it took me about a year to finish it.

The Annapolis Valley of Nova Scotia is rich in folklore about Glooscap, the mighty god of the Mi'kmaq people. The Mi'kmaq believe that Glooscap is a teacher, protector, prophet, and transformer of the landscape who is responsible for creating many of the rock formations and islands around Nova Scotia.

Although he has gone away now, the Mi'kmaq believe Glooscap will return if they are ever in dire need.

I remembered a project from my high school days on aboriginal picture writing, and I used many of those symbols in the design of this rug. Other designs in the rug are typical of aboriginal beadwork and quillwork, and I used them to fill in the background and link the symbols together.

The brown background in the outside border provides a setting for the grey, gold, red, and blue step pattern that echoes the colours found throughout the rug. In the next band the three-pronged design in the corner—the symbol for feathers—is hooked in shades of reddish brown and rust. I repeated this colour scheme in the eagle, symbolic of the power of Glooscap and his friendship with birds and animals. The adjacent sign stands for a bird, and the three triangles sitting atop each other

represent corn—i.e. a bird eating corn. I hooked both these motifs in shades of white and gold.

In the next band I shaded the arrowheads in grey and blue plaid and the jagged lightning in white, blue, and black. At the sides, I used rust and green to make up the human figures of man and woman. In the next band I used a blue background to show up the round black and white shapes that are symbolic of day and night. My centre panel has a gold background at either end featuring black birds (ravens) in flight. I hooked the triangles in the centre using all the colours of the rug and hooked a light grey background behind the triangles for contrast.

I used commercial dyes in addition to onion skins to achieve colours that resemble the natural vegetable dyes the Mi'kmaq would have used.

Maori

42″ × 72″
1970

This rug was inspired by a *National Geographic* article on the aboriginal tribes of New Guinea. The designs on their ceremonial huts were fascinating.

For the background I used the wool from green coats, first removing as much colour as possible. Then I over-dyed it with an Egyptian red colour, giving the rug a muted red background that made it look aged from the start. It would have had quite a different look with more brilliant colours.

The Birds

49″ × 34″
1989

───────────────

This rug came about because of a remark by a woman from Blandford, Nova Scotia. She said her mother had kept a notebook of "written patterns." Now, I had seen old templates and patterns drawn on paper, but what did she mean by written patterns? I decided to try "writing" a pattern of my own, devising a counting method, much as you would in counted thread embroidery.

I divided my rug warp backing with a horizontal and a vertical centre line. Starting at the centre line along the width, I worked toward the corner, hooking in my pattern every other stitch in every other row. I had to use a uniform width of cut wool, so that the hooking remained even and precise.

When I neared the corner I worked the two, the side and the end, to meet and form a pattern, writing all this information down as I went along. I then had one-quarter of my rug hooked and recorded! By working the other three quarters out from the centre lines I could complete my design from my written notes. The centre is simply hooked two across and two down, to form a diagonal pattern with controlled colours.

When I was almost finished, a visitor told me of a Navajo rug she had seen in the American southwest. She pointed out that a line extended from the centre to the outer edge of the rug that "allowed the spirit to go free." I loved this idea and added it to my piece, too.

A LIFETIME OF RUG-HOOKING

Man, Bird, and Beast

42″ × 24″
1972

———————————————————

This depiction of man, bird, and beast is executed in fairly traditional colours. The hanging is done as a double panel, with the background panel suggesting a prairie sunset, and the man, bird, and beast, like a mini totem pole, hanging from the same rod at the top.

The fringe may be a bit unusual. I used the cut woollen strips left from my hooking and knotted them along the sides and bottom edges. I think they're in keeping with the total concept of the piece.

STAIR RUNNERS: EXQUISITE ELEVATIONS

Hand-hooked stair runners or stair treads are a wonderful addition to any home. However, standing at the bottom of the steps and looking up can be daunting when you think about hooking them.

Hooking a stair runner is a commitment of many months, but it seems to go along quite quickly because they are fairly narrow. I would rather hook a runner, because the treads take a lot of finishing along all edges. I would prefer to do the extra hooking and just hem back the outer edge.

Our daughter Mary started a wonderful stair runner with a very interesting story and theme, but on the steps the pattern was completely broken up and lost its meaning. She hooked seven feet before deciding that it should become a lovely floor to ceiling hanging instead. If you have a complicated pattern, make sure it will flow as it climbs the stairs.

Stewart Stair Treads

1979

When I worked on this set of stair treads, I put a great deal of thought into the house they were going into, the people who lived there, and the town of Mahone Bay where this house has stood for so many years. Gradually I created a story and it became my Legend of the Stair Treads. Here it is:

Because the Stewart house is old and the steps are very worn, each tread was a different depth and had to be measured carefully. Every step had to be given its own number and

you can see I hooked that number in the lower right hand corner of each tread. Since the treads were now all numbered, it stood to reason that letters could be used, too, so I assigned letters to all the risers, and as these letters climb up the stairs they each relate their own interesting story.

The first riser has the letter A. I hooked in images of acorns, because

they are the fruit of the mighty oak, a steadfast tree standing tall in our forests in Nova Scotia. I also hooked in the year 1979, because it was the 225th anniversary of the town of Mahone Bay. I hooked my name, too, as the humble artist of this work.

The very first step is the letter B, the riser above it is C, the next step is D, and so on. I hooked colourful treads for each step. The riser with the letter C stands for Carolyn Stewart, who commissioned these treads to be hooked and who so imaginatively decorated this home. It also depicts the cherries that we enjoy from our trees, which have beautiful white blossoms in the springtime.

The next riser is E and I hooked the Evening Star, a star to wish on. The letter G in the next riser's upper left-hand corner stands for Gordon Stewart, whose labours restored this beautiful home. I hooked a picture of those splendid and distinctive birds, our Canada Geese. The letter I on the next riser inspired me to hook Indian paintbrush, the brilliant flower of our summer fields.

K is a very special picture. It is of a little girl named Kimberley Stewart and her initial is in the upper left-hand corner. She's dressed in blue, a colour her grandmother especially favours.

Mahone Bay is represented in the next riser (M) so I hooked that well-known image of the three churches you see when you enter the town along the bay. Look closely for the bird's nest in one of the trees—my granddaughter was watching as I hooked that particular day and she whispered that I should hide a nest in the tree.

O, on the next riser, is Our Home, referring to this house that had been carefully and lovingly restored and was the Stewart family's haven and pride.

For the riser Q I hooked the quail, the native bird of our forests and fields that comes to our back doors for food in the deep snows of winter. And S is for the sailboats that glide past the front door of this house in the glorious days of summer.

That takes us to the top of the stairs, but my legend is not quite finished. When you're at the top of these stairs looking down, you can see in the treads all the colours of the forest floor when you go for a walk on a crisp autumn day. I hooked the treads thinking about the scarlets, golds, and corals of maple leaves; the rusts and browns of oak leaves and pine needles; the greys of lichens and stones; the greens of moss and grass; and the reds and purples of berries.

As I hooked all of these colours, I thought of all the people who are part of these stair treads and risers. The very nature of rug hooking is to use discarded woolens from garments that are no longer useful, so my materials had to come from many people. I washed the woolens and sorted them; some were used in the colours I found them, but I dyed others to suit the design. When you think about it, just about every colour came from a different person, so that many, many people are represented in this work. We all came together to make these stair treads for this gracious old home in Mahone Bay.

Poppies by the Brook, and Companion

Stair runner with separate companion rug for bottom of the stairs
2.5 feet × 21 feet
1989

Our stairs at home are old, steep, and narrow, so I hooked this runner for them that I call "Poppies

by the Brook." It took me a year to complete.

People had slipped and fallen on our steep steps in the past, but since the runner was installed no one has fallen, and if they did, it would at least be a softer landing. When our dog Taz was a puppy he didn't know how to get down the stairs and they terrified him. Now he travels up or down without hesitation.

The idea for this stair runner came from my memory of flowers nodding by the brook and the water as it rushed along beside them. The actual flowers were wild irises and wild roses and violets, but I chose to use my favourite poppies instead and drew them freehand in a random way along the border of the stair runner. I filled them in with leaves and then hooked the water in a flowing way, keeping the colours darker beneath

the flowers and lighter through the centre of the runner.

I outlined all the recognizable forms in black as my grandmother would have done, and I used an army blanket of khaki colour to hook the outside border. Army blankets were used after both world wars, and I had read somewhere that "colour on mud sings." It's true. Yucky colours beneath bright colours make the bright reds, golds, and greens come alive.

At one point I broke the flower pattern along the edge and I remember consciously leaving it, perhaps to better achieve a free-flowing effect. Or perhaps it allowed the spirit to go free. To my surprise when this piece was put in place on the stairs, it became a beautiful waterfall!

A small hallway at the bottom of the stairs seemed to need a rug, so I worked out a companion rug with a wide border—a squiggly centre picking up the light shades from the treads, and random poppies on top.

THE SAGA OF A STAIR RUNNER

Stair runner hooked for the Wolter house, 1995

When Helmut and Edith Wolter purchased a very dilapidated Nova Scotia house in the spring of 1989, friends scratched their heads and wondered what this otherwise intelligent couple was thinking. The last resident of the house had been a horse and the living room had been used to store its hay. The floors were badly battered and wasps had built a nest behind the plaster, between the studding. Over many years the nest had filled the space from floor to ceiling like gray parchment.

It was a sound old house but it needed total restoration, starting with a new foundation through to new plumbing and heating. Helmut and Edith had a will to restore this forsaken old house to its original, simple beauty. Mouldings were carefully removed, stripped of many layers of paint, and then put back in their original places. The house was newly insulated against the winter winds of their hilltop location, and new double-glazed windows were installed throughout. The walls were finished with plasterboard and the old floors were sanded to bring out their beautiful patina.

Month after month they went daily to their task, back and forth on a ferry across the LaHave River. They would move in when the house was weathertight and a heating system had been installed. The work continued. Months turned into years. Finishing touches finally brought it to life.

The most time-consuming project of all was left until last. It was the restoration of the staircase near the front entryway, with a stained glass window above its landing. The steps were broken and had to be replaced. Any existing wood that could be saved was painstakingly stripped of paint and sanded down, then stained and varnished and reused.

Perhaps it was fortunate that, because of the time it would have taken to refinish them, the spindles, rails, and newel posts were missing. Helmut hired a local craftsman to replace the simple one-by-one-inch spindles and install a new railing up to the landing, neatly turning and continuing to the top of the stair and along the upper hallway.

When they saw the finished staircase, they knew the perfect finishing touch to the steps and to the whole restoration project would be a hand-hooked stair runner. Many of their friends hooked rugs and both Edith and Helmut loved the beauty of design and colour possible in hand-hooked creations. But since neither of them hooked, the task seemed monumental.

Helmut had an idea: what fun it would be if their friends would each contribute a hooked riser to the project! His idea was enthusiastically embraced by friends who were experienced hookers and also by friends who wanted to learn and take part. It was agreed that it would be even more exciting if each person designed and hooked his or her own design, independently of each other and also as a surprise to their friends, the Wolters.

The idea was adopted, but it presented specific problems that made more work for the Wolters at the final stages because all the separate pieces had to be joined to hooked treads and eventually joined, piece by piece, into a long runner to cover the entire flight of stairs.

Helmut had been a surgeon in his native Germany and volunteered to stitch the pieces together as they were completed, but the gentle touch of a surgeon's hand wasn't quite what was needed to tightly bind all the pieces together with seams strong enough to withstand the wear and tear of years of use. Another consideration was assembling the pieces together in the best way possible to show off their colour and design, which couldn't be done until all the pieces were complete.

Friends who wanted to be included but had never hooked before were enrolled in a class, along with Helmut and Edith. A teacher was hired to come to the house and the basics were taught in two sessions. Helmut made lap frames for each student and everyone was provided with linen backing, hooks, and woolen hooking materials. Some experienced hookers also hooked a tread after they had finished their riser, and then Helmut and Edith filled in with the necessary treads to complete the job. As it turned out, there were more people wanting to participate than there were steps to cover.

As the finished pieces started to trickle in, the Wolters realized what an interesting project they had conceived. Agnes hooked the scene of the bay and a small island, as seen from the window of the house the Wolters had rented since moving to Nova Scotia. Their daughter-in-law, Wanda, hooked the colourful red, yellow, and green peppers she grows for the Farmer's Market. Helmut depicted in amazing detail the Cologne Cathedral of his hometown

The Wolter stair runner on display at the DesBrisay Museum, 1995

in Germany, the Heidelberg Gate, and their farm in Quebec. I hooked the pattern of the wasps' nest found in the wall as a neutral piece for the landing. My husband Ron grows special chickens that lay green eggs, but arthritis made hooking too difficult for him, so Edith hooked the riser. She gives him credit with his name embroidered along the border, as are the others.

Marilyn hooked card symbols to remind Helmut and Edith of the many canasta games enjoyed together on winter evenings, and Gwen did a scene of the couple's Quebec farm in more detail. Mary and Earl hooked

the boat they shared for rides, cutting through the water around the islands, and Helmut and Edith's daughter Simone hooked the playful dolphins, her favourites.

Vita designed brown-eyed Susans, which grow abundantly in Edith's wild garden around the house, and Doris W. adapted an abstract scene with an airborne cow from a painting by Franz Marc. Joan, a local artist, hooked seagulls in flight against a summer sky. Marbie finished the runner with Chippy, the Wolters' fourteen-year-old cat lounging on the top of the steps with mice peeping at her from both sides.

The year 1995 had been designated the "Year of the Hooked Mat" by the province of Nova Scotia and this supplied the impetus to finish the runner. A deadline was set for finished work to be submitted and Edith began the daunting task of hand-stitching treads to risers and risers to treads, on and on up the staircase. A one-and-a-half-inch border had been allowed for and was then hooked around the entire runner to bring it all together. The result is a joyful, eclectic mix of colour and design, each riser a story in itself. The fisherman next door came over to see it and said: "Wow! It must be worth a million dollars!" Well, maybe it is. Then again, maybe it's priceless.

The whole project was complete by the end of June and it became the highlight of the rug-hooking exhibition at the DesBrisay Museum in Bridgewater, a national exhibition centre. Almost four thousand people saw it.

When the exhibition was dismantled, the runner was finally brought home and installed. As a special thank you to everyone, Edith and Helmut invited all hands to a fine dinner at the Lion Inn in Lunenburg. Following dinner, the party moved to the Wolters' home for the unveiling, and a toast was proposed to a job well done.

Wasps' Nest

24" × 33"
1994

This is the rug I hooked for the Wolters' stair treads, for the landing where the stairway turns. I designed it from a photo taken before renovations began. Wasps had built solid hives between the studding in the walls of the living room where the plaster had fallen away. The colours probably came from wallpapers nearby. The hives were a most interesting preservation of the history of that old house.

OLD DOG, NEW TRICKS: THE EATON EDGE

Our daughter Mary repairs and restores precious hand-hooked rugs. When she first started, she had a young family and this work provided added income that allowed her to stay at home with her children. I admire her patience when she tackles some rather hopeless rugs and brings them back to their use and beauty. What began as a small business has now become something quite different for Mary, and her attitude toward this work has changed. Now she truly appreciates the old rugs she handles, and gets excited when a particularly beautiful one comes through her door and is repairable. She feels it's very special if she can bring these heirloom pieces back into circulation, and I agree with her. Because of the problems she's had to solve with these older rugs over the years, I've learned a lot from her perspective as a restorer.

The first problem Mary has encountered is in the choice of backing, which can cause the rug to be beyond repair. One particular group of rugs came to Mary that were absolutely beautiful and original in their designs. They were probably hooked before 1900 by someone very artistic. The only thing wrong with them was the backing. The hooking itself was of good wool and very sound.

The burlap had become so brittle with age that you could put your finger through the rug and the burlap would break away, easily and tragically. As Mary repaired one section, the piece next to it would break away and eventually she had to give up in frustration. It was impossible to save those beautiful rugs, just because of their backing. This isn't always the case, but it is often the problem. Her customer was very disappointed.

You may think that a rug over one hundred years old has outlived its usefulness, but I don't agree, especially if a choice of backing can make the difference. Mary Sheppard Burton convinced me years ago of the fine qualities of linen as a foundation for our hooked rugs, and Mary Klotz of Forestheart Studio published excellent research comparing linen to burlap in the March–April 1990 issue of *Rug Hooking Magazine*.

Here in Nova Scotia, the Museum of Natural History in Halifax has a fine collection of old Nova Scotia mats, the oldest of which are hooked on homespun flax (linen). They predate burlap and in relative terms they're in better condition because of the backing material.

An early source of foundation material was the "bag burlap" used for sacks of grain for livestock. It was of poor quality, but was available and useful to recycle for mat bottoms for hooked rugs. Thrifty women wanted rugs for cold floors, and saved worn out clothing to hook them with. The women were happy to get whatever was available for backing material.

Today, linen specially woven for hooked rugs is available to us, and is the much-preferred material for the foundation of our beautiful workmanship.

The second problem is the lack of identification on almost every rug that Mary has ever had to repair. There is no name, not even an initial, and they are not dated. The maker had no idea how important this information would be in the history of the rug, or how significant it would be to those of us who try to identify and record these survivors.

It's a great accomplishment to finish a rug. If you are a rug hooker, you know all too well how much time and thought and energy and knowledge and artistry go into these creations. Be proud of your efforts. Sign and date them. Your children and future generations will cherish them for many years to come. Your signature can become part of your design and be very subtly added to your work.

The third problem Mary must solve in older rugs is the most common of all—refinishing the worn edges,

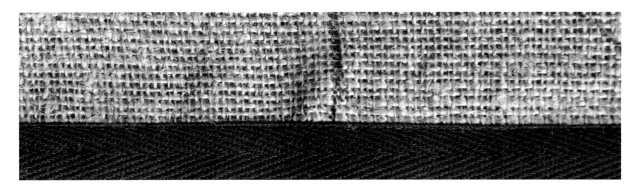

which show wear more quickly than the rest of the rug. An early method was to roll the burlap along the outer edge of a completed rug, to the underside, and to add a few rows of hooking. The loops pulled through both layers. Done. Another method was to simply turn the burlap at the edge of a finished mat to the reverse side and hem it back. In both cases, the burlap at the perimeter of the rug became exposed to light and became brittle fairly quickly, requiring costly repairs. (Thank goodness we don't do that any longer.)

Another common practice was to crochet around the outer edge of the mat bottom before beginning to hook, usually with black yarn. It was then laced into mat bars and the rug was "finished" as soon as it was hooked.

Another popular way to finish a rug is by whipping the edge. I am certainly no authority on this, but I did try it once, several years ago, on *The Old Gent Himself*. The rug was an odd shape, but I trimmed the backing material to within a few inches of the finished rug, and ran a length of cording next to the hooking on the reverse side. Then I rolled the backing material over the cording and, with black yarn and a tapestry needle, proceeded to cover the edge with a whipping stitch, over and over, closely stitching to cover the backing, padded with cording.

I worked at this for a few hours, and thought about what I was doing. Was that needle pulling yarn over and over and over again, all around my rug, really the way to go? It looked good, but I felt it was weakening my piece at the very place where it was most vulnerable to wear. I had only whipped a few feet and decided this was not the best edge for the sake of my rug. I painstakingly took it all out, and I haven't tried it again, although it is a favourite method for many hookers. It is a relatively recent method of finishing, but I wonder how it will stand the test of time?

THE EATON EDGE

When I learned to hook from Mrs. Withrow in 1961, we sewed binding onto our pattern at the beginning, then hooked our rug. We hemmed the binding back when we were finished. (The row of hooking next to the binding was hooked low; in this way the edge was tapered and fairly durable.) Very simple. I've found it to be as good as any finish for my rugs over the years. But I've been looking for a better way. And, quite by accident, I found it.

Before Christmas 2000, I had finished a commissioned piece that was to be a wall hanging. I wanted the border to simulate a frame in some way. Thinking the piece would be lit from above, I used reverse hooking in some rows in the border to give depth and a feeling of the moulding of a wooden frame. Planning to hook the outside row very low, I hooked it from the back of the piece (reverse hooking) as close as possible to the lines of stitching used when applying the binding. When the hooking was

finished and I tried to turn back the binding, I had stumbled upon the very technique I had been looking for to finish a rug. And it's so simple. I had the low row of hooking at the edge, and the binding wrapped around the reverse loops to provide padding and to take the wear of the rug. I was satisfied with it, especially as a finish for a rug for the floor.

The binding should match or complement the colours in the hooking at the edge of the rug, because it will be visible. When you turn it toward the back to hem it, it will wrap around the loops of that last row of hooking and those loops will pad the binding as though a piece of cording had been inserted. The binding will therefore project beyond the edge of the rug and will take the wear and tear of your rug for extended years.

What will I name this discovery? Of course! "The Eaton Edge."

I demonstrated this at a hook-in at Smith Cove, and one lady jumped to her feet. "No more whipping?"

"That's right," I said.

I got a standing ovation.

1 Sew binding onto the linen (or other backing material) at a line drawn at the perimeter of your rug. Follow instructions, but do note that the right-angle corners will stick up. This is as it should be and they will mitre back into place when hemmed.

Instructions for Hookers

There are four easy steps to achieve this method of finishing a rug.

1 Draw a line around the perimeter of your backing before you start to hook. This will be the size of your rug. Lay the binding along this line on the top side, and top stitch very closely along the very edge of your tape. When you come to a corner, put your machine needle into the fabric and turn the piece forty-five degrees to make a right angle. The binding will stand up straight. This may seem difficult at first, but gets easier with practice. Continue to stitch to the next corner, turn, and continue. When you have stitched on the binding all the way around, cut the binding an inch longer, turn it back half an inch, and overlap the tape where you began.

2 Turn your foundation material to the wrong, or back, side and stretch it onto your frame. You'll see your row of stitching. Hook one row of your border colour or the colour of your binding in the very next row of the backing—in other words, as close as possible. I like a #6 width for this (no smaller than that). Hook this row all the way around the edge, clipping your ends the height of your loops. This is reverse hooking.

3 Remove it from the frame, turn it over, and stretch it on the frame again, top side up. Now your finish work is almost done. Hook your entire rug.

4 Press your finished rug with a hot iron and a damp cotton cloth to steam it nice and smooth. Hem back the binding. Fold back carefully over the reverse-hooked loops and hem into place with good, strong thread. Press the edge again if necessary, and you're all set. Your work is done. Enjoy!

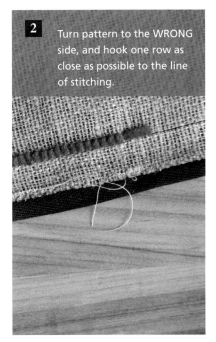

2 Turn pattern to the WRONG side, and hook one row as close as possible to the line of stitching.

3 Turn your rug over to the right side and hook the entire rug. Now all you have to do is hem back the binding.

THE PLEASURE OF WORKING IN GROUPS

I started hooking fifty years ago in 1961. Why didn't I start sooner? I've hooked a few hundred rugs and many smaller projects, like hangings, runners, coasters, and chair covers, but there are still many more rug ideas swirling around in my head.

My most ambitious rug took seven years to complete. It was the saph rug I hooked of my family, using a fine #3 cut, outlining motifs and then hooking the entire 40-inch by 112-inch rug horizontally, to simulate the weaving of traditional oriental rugs. This was a true commitment and a genuine discipline.

Every one of those fifty years of hooking have been rewarding, and I have certainly received recognition for my efforts. I've demonstrated at fairs and exhibitions and museums countless times, and taught many

courses in rug schools, high schools, historic homes, community halls, living rooms, kitchens, patios, and basement rec rooms. I've exhibited extensively in solo and groups shows locally and from Massachusetts to Montreal. But now, sharing what I've come to know about our craft at weekly hook-ins is all the "teaching" I want to do.

In all my years of teaching, I taught what I had been taught by excellent teachers—Mrs. Withrow, our own Nova Scotia rug school teachers, and the instructors at courses in Decorah, Iowa; Quail Hill, Maine; and other U.S. centres. I learned to dye materials in many different ways and was given many rules to follow. Today, if a beginner comes to me, I have a selection of hooks for her to choose from. I show her how to stretch her

backing material on a simple frame, how to cut her fabric into strips, how to pull a loop through her linen, and then I let her go. I am positively amazed to see what can be done without a lot of rules to follow.

Rug-hooking groups are important in so many ways to encourage and nurture our efforts. We feed off each other and help solve problems and generate ideas. Some groups start with show and tell and the members suggest solutions when needed, or offer encouragement, which is always needed. Even women who aren't "joiners" find the groups helpful and fun. Different points of view give different options for a hooker, helping with problems of design or colour she can't seem to solve on her own. We keep each other updated on events, articles in magazines and newspapers, books, and gatherings in neighbouring communities.

My involvement in groups began when I stopped teaching rug hooking and needed a way to stay in touch with other hookers. In the early years I really enjoyed a group that met at Mrs. Oickle's Green Bay Antiques. She welcomed us each week with two full pots of coffee and we loved her home amid beautiful antiques. This group eventually evolved into the "Monday Group."

A few years ago at one of our meetings we talked about being original in our rugs, even "jumping out of the box." A number of us formed a spin-off group called the "Square Zebras." I knew just the right person to "kick off" this new group—

Judith Dalegret from Montreal. She summers in Nova Scotia and we met with her and several rug hookers she knew from the Sandy Cove and Smith's Cove area. We had an inspiring meeting and came up with the following mission statement:

"The Square Zebras is an interactive group of rug hookers having fun together, not necessarily hooking rugs but developing the confidence, artistic skills, and ideas of each individual through discussion, lectures, and visits to and from other artists and artisans. In so doing, helping each to progress beyond the traditional roots of rug hooking and develop their own skills, talents, abilities, styles, and their own designs."

One of the first major endeavours of the Square Zebras was a rug-hooking exhibition at our local LaHave Islands Marine Museum in 2007. We called the show "Fresh Off the Hook" and it proved to be very successful. We had calendars made of the fourteen rugs submitted and donated a portion of calendar sales to the museum.

Besides all of this, there is another group that meets at the Hebbville Fire Department hall each Thursday, and yet another gathering on Tuesday afternoons at a beautiful church in Rose Bay. Spruce Top Rug-Hooking Studio and Encompassing Design both welcome regular hook-ins at their shops, too. All this within a half-hour of my home.

But my favourite group has to be the one that meets once a month and has named itself "Doris's Girls." (This is the group that sent me off to Japan.) We have met and hooked together every single month since November 1979. We first met in October of that year when I was teaching a full week of hooking lessons at the DesBrisay Museum in Bridgewater and they were my students.

At our last class of this course, I told them the best way to keep going and expand their interest in hooking

was to meet regularly every month. I invited them to my house for that first November meeting in 1979. We have become best friends, close friends, with utter respect for each other. The most incredible thing has happened. Our daughters have joined us, so we have a new generation of rug hookers with us at our monthly meetings.

Perhaps the greatest achievement, with the most meaningful effect on rug hooking in the province, was the formation of the Rug Hooking Guild of Nova Scotia. The guild is the umbrella over all of us. It sponsors two rug schools per year, each offering a week of instruction, with qualified teachers, in several categories. We are so lucky in Nova Scotia to have strong support and instruction in what we love to do. There is no end to the lessons we'll learn from this vibrant fibre art.

During the 1970s, I was teaching in several areas of the province, giving workshops and teaching full ten-week courses in Dartmouth, Halifax, Canning, Petite Riviere, New Ross, and Bridgewater. This put me in a unique position to watch the growth of our rug-hooking tradition and I was excited by the enthusiasm and artistry I found everywhere. There were opportunities to exhibit work in local fire halls and museums, and I felt if we were better organized as a provincial group, there would be even more opportunities to grow and develop.

Pockets of rug hookers were forming groups from Middleton to Canning in the Valley, along the South Shore, in Halifax, Dartmouth, and Cape Breton—basically wherever there were teachers. I asked each area to send two delegates to a meeting at the Forties Community Centre in the middle of the province for a discussion and to make a decision as to whether a provincial guild should be formed. The response was unani-

mous in favour of the idea and the Rug Hooking Guild of Nova Scotia was born.

I became honorary president and we elected a full slate of officers, appointed directors to represent each area, and formed committees to proceed with our agenda. Our first full meeting took place the next month in Port Williams, and we presented Mrs. Edna Withrow of Wolfville with our first Life Membership. We planned semi-annual meetings for spring and fall, to take place in different parts of the province. Because of the travel involved and because there was so much to learn, these meetings also included programs and instruction. Our first major project was the proposal to hold an annual rug-hooking school and a committee was formed to organize this ambitious event.

We were successful in receiving a grant from the Province of Nova Scotia, which enabled me to travel to Ontario, where successful schools were already being held each year. Their president spent a few days with me and we hired teachers from their organization and came up with interesting courses to offer, from a teacher-training course to designing, shading, and dyeing, to classes in primitive and oriental design. This was all very exciting. We had good teaching staff and our committee did an excellent job carrying out our mandate.

From the beginning our school was so successful that we didn't have to return to the government for further funding. Indeed, we now conduct a school in May and one in September, with attendance from across North America.

New Brunswick and Prince Edward Island are also members of our guild and all three provinces have several women who have become qualified rug-hooking teachers and present courses at our schools. These are proud achievements for all of us.

APPENDIX: HOOKER'S SLUSH

This is a recipe given to me years ago by Kaye Magwood of Bridgetown, Nova Scotia. It's always on tap and very refreshing.

   1 pint gin
   1/2 cup cherry brandy
   1/2 cup grenadine
   1/2 cup lemon juice
   1 small can frozen lemonade
   6 oz. juice from maraschino
      cherries
   19 oz. can pineapple juice
   1/2 cup sugar
   4 cups water

Mix everything together. Freeze.

To serve, stir well, mixing bottom concentration with top ice.

Fill your glass half full, add Sprite or 7-Up, stir, and serve with a straw.